THE BASICS OF GENETICS

CORE CONCEPTS

THE BASICS OF GENETICS

ANNE WANJIE, EDITOR

ROSEN
PUBLISHING®
New York

This edition published in 2014 by:

The Rosen Publishing Group, Inc.
29 East 21st Street
New York, NY 10010

Additional end matter copyright © 2014 by The Rosen Publishing
Group, Inc.

Library of Congress Cataloging-in-Publication Data

Wanjie, Anne.
The Basics of genetics/by Anne Wanjie.
  p. cm.—(Core concepts)
Includes bibliographical references and index.
ISBN 978-1-4777-0552-0 (library binding)
1. Genetics—Juvenile literature. I. Title.
QH437.5 W36 2014
576.5—d23

Manufactured in the United States of America

CPSIA Compliance Information: Batch #S13YA: For further information, contact Rosen Publishing,
New York, New York, at 1-800-237-9932.

© 2004 Brown Bear Books Ltd.

CONTENTS

CHAPTER ONE

GENETICS: THE STUDY OF HEREDITY

What determines your height, hair color, ear shape, blood type, and every other feature of your body? The answer lies in your genes.

Everything about you, from the way you look to how your body functions, is controlled by genes. Genes are packets of information that form a code. You inherited your genes from your mom and

Features such as the children's eye and hair color depend on genes received from their mom and dad, although the environment in which they grow up can affect characteristics such as height and weight.

dad. Genes occur on stretches of long chemicals called deoxyribonucleic acid, or DNA. Genetics is the study of how genes pass through the generations and the role of DNA and other chemicals.

Most cells in your body have a control center called a nucleus. The nucleus contains all the genes needed to make your body and keep it working. An organism's complete set of genes is called its genome. DNA carrying the genes is organized into structures called chromosomes. Every species has a fixed number of chromosomes—humans have 46, for example.

DNA: AN IMPORTANT MOLECULE

Genes are sequences of chemicals called bases on a very special molecule—DNA. Life as we know it could not exist without DNA. Genes on a DNA molecule work by driving the production of chemicals called proteins in the cell. Proteins may be products such as hormones. Proteins also include enzymes, without which chemical reactions inside the body could not take place. To make proteins using DNA, a similar chemical, RNA, is needed.

GENETIC VARIATION

Take a look at the other children in your class. Why are there several different hair colors? Hair color is produced by pigments inside the hairs. Pigments are made by chemical reactions inside cells. Different pigments are made by different reactions, and each needs the help of an enzyme. People with different hair colors have different combinations of genes. The various combinations lead to the production of different enzymes.

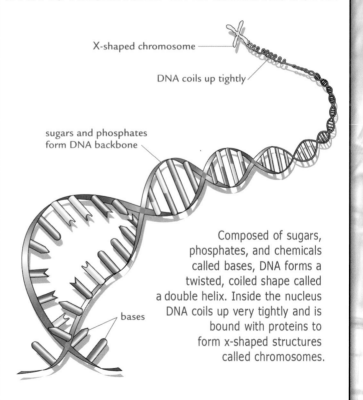

DNA IS PACKAGED IN A CHROMOSOME

X-shaped chromosome

DNA coils up tightly

sugars and phosphates form DNA backbone

bases

Composed of sugars, phosphates, and chemicals called bases, DNA forms a twisted, coiled shape called a double helix. Inside the nucleus DNA coils up very tightly and is bound with proteins to form x-shaped structures called chromosomes.

A scientist looks at a person's DNA profile. Advances in our understanding of genetics allow scientists to carry out DNA finger-printing, a valuable technique in police work as well as in biological research.

INHERITING TRAITS

Half of the 46 chromosomes inside each cell in your body are provided by your mom; the other half come from your dad. Male sex cells, or sperm, carry one set of chromosomes. Female sex cells, or eggs, carry the other. A sperm and an egg come together in a process called fertilization. That forms a cell called a zygote. You and everybody else started life as a zygote. The chromosome sets provided by your parents began to work together there. That's what makes you you.

The genes carried on the chromo-somes tell your cells what color your eyes are and what size your nose is; every feature of your body is shaped by genes. Each feature, though, is coded for by two versions of a gene, one from your mother and one from your father. The paired genes are called alleles. Sometimes both alleles are the same, but different versions may be present. How does the body know which set of genetic instructions to follow?

The answer is that some alleles are dominant: The trait they code for is always shown when the alleles are present. Other alleles are recessive. Recessive alleles only come into effect in the absence of dominant alleles.

HEREDITY VS. ENVIRONMENT

Not every feature is exclusively deter-mined by genes—some are affected by the environment. For example, weight can be affected by how many calories a person eats and how much exercise they do. Similarly, characteristics such as intelligence and criminal tendencies might be linked to genes, but they may also be affected by how an individual was raised. So which is more important—genes or the environment?

COPYING AND DIVIDING

After the zygote that would become you was formed, the cells divided again and again. This cell division continued as you developed. Some types of cells stopped dividing soon after you were born. Others will divide for the rest of your life, to repair wounds, for example. When a cell divides, the new cells it creates need new sets of chromosomes.

A process called mitosis creates accurate DNA copies that go from cell to cell. That ensures every cell in your body has the same set of genes to work with.

Things are different when the sex cells are being made. Like other cells, sex cells form through cell division, and DNA copies need to be made. However, the resulting sex cells must have only 23 chromosomes rather than 46. Also, the DNA is mixed up a little to make new combinations of genes, increasing genetic diversity. The process of sex cell production is called meiosis.

GENE REGULATION

Almost every cell in your body has the same set of genes. That is because DNA is copied every time a cell divides. But how can cells, such as muscle cells and brain cells, end up doing different jobs? Genes are switched on or off depending on where they are in the body, and what stage in their development they have reached. So, muscle cells contract, and brain cells carry nerve impulses despite their having identical genes.

ADVANCES IN BIOTECHNOLOGY

Scientists use their knowledge of genetics to change the characteristics of organisms. Plants and animals can be selectively bred for useful feature. In recent years crops and animals have been genetically modified (altered) to protect against pests or to increase yields. Genetically modified organisms are also useful in medicine, in the production of the hormone insulin. Understanding inheritance helps physicians figure out the likelihood of genetic disorders such as hemophilia occurring.

Further advances have followed since the completion of the Human Genome Project (HGP) in April 2003. It saw the mapping of every human gene—an invaluable tool for medical researchers.

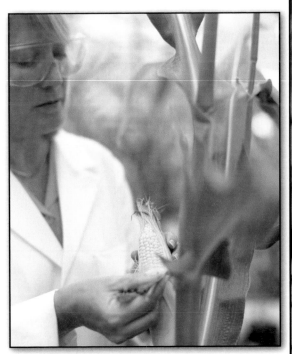

A researcher examines an ear of genetically modified corn.

CHAPTER TWO

PRINCIPLES OF INHERITANCE

Monk and botanist Gregor Mendel is often remembered as the father of genetics.

Have you ever wondered why you look more like members of your family than your friends at school? Or why a cat never gives birth to a dog? The answers lie in the study of inheritance. Characteristics pass from parents to young in the form of genes. Scientists now know that genes are carried on stretches of deoxyribonucleic acid, or DNA, molecules.

The way characteristics move between generations is now well understood. But before the late 19th century inheritance was mysterious. The man who figured out how inheritance worked was an Austrian monk called Gregor Mendel (1822–1884).

GARDEN EXPERIMENTS

Mendel carried out lots of experiments in the gardens of his abbey. He crossed (bred) different garden pea varieties. They had traits, such as flower color or

AN EARLY THEORY

Mendel found the discoveries of some other scientists useful in his work. German botanist Josef Gottlieb Kölreuter (1733–1806) showed that parents contributed equally to the features of their young. However, what the parents were actually contributing remained unknown. Before the rediscovery of Mendel's work scientists like Charles Darwin (1809–1882) suggested that features could blend like mixtures of paint. So, crossing a red flower and a blue flower would lead to a blend of the two—in this case, purple flowers. Blending was not the answer, however, since it would cause any diversity to swiftly disappear.

seed shape, that were easy to identify and catalog. Eggs inside female flowers are fertilized by pollen, a powder that contains sex cells released by male flowers. Fertilized eggs develop into seeds. Using a fine brush to transfer the pollen, Mendel could cross two plants or make a plant self-pollinate (fertilize itself).

The diagram shows what happened in one of Mendel's experiments. He crossed a pea with purple flowers with a white-flowered plant. The resulting seeds (called the F1 generation) were planted. All the young grew to have purple flowers.

Mendel then self-pollinated the F1 flowers. Of these young (the F2 generation) three-quarters had purple flowers. But one-quarter had white flowers, just like one of their grandparents. What on earth was going on?

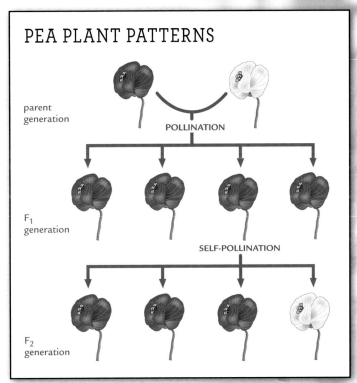

PEA PLANT PATTERNS

parent generation

POLLINATION

F₁ generation

SELF-POLLINATION

F₂ generation

EXPLAINING THE RESULTS

Mendel suggested that the particles responsible for passing on traits such as flower color occurred in pairs. One particle was contributed by each parent plant.

HOW DO PUNNETT SQUARES WORK?

Punnett squares give a simple way to figure out the genotypes of the young, provided you know what the genotypes of the parents are. To fill in a Punnett square, take the genotype of the parents, and separate the alleles for each gene. That reflects the way alleles split in sex cell formation. Then write all the male sex cell alleles on one side of the Punnett square and all the female sex cell alleles on the other. Adding one to the other in the Punnett square gives all the possible genotypes of the young.

This tells you what the young will look like, and in what proportions the resulting phenotypes are likely to occur.

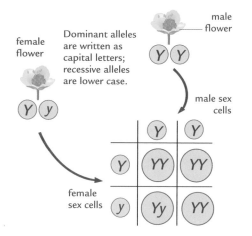

Alleles pass randomly from each parent to the young. The Punnett square shows the allele combinations and in what proportions they occur. Here, three-quarters of the young are YY, and the rest are Yy.

DIAGRAMMING MENDEL'S RESULTS

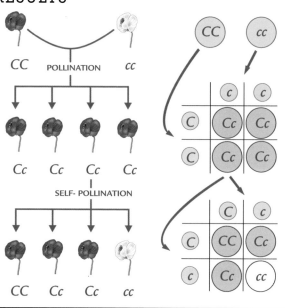

Furthermore, he suggested that these particles separate from one another during the formation of sex cells (in this case the eggs and pollen). So each sex cell contained one particle. But the resulting young had two particles, since two sex cells fuse to form young. Mendel's inheritance particle is now called a gene. In the flower color experiment Mendel reasoned that the parent plants with purple flowers had two similar versions of a gene—let's label them CC. The white-flowered plants had two different versions, cc. Each

GENOTYPE AND PHENOTYPE

"Genotype" and "phenotype" are important terms. The genotype is the makeup of genes inside an organism. The phenotype is all the outward, observable characteristics of an organism, as coded for by its genotype. There are two possible genotypes that lead to the purple-flowered phenotype in peas. They are CC and Cc.

Imagine that an allele, E, codes for chest feather color. The genotype for the chest feathers of this cardinal may be thought of as EE or Ee. Red feather coloration is the single phenotype linked to both of these combinations of alleles.

HOMOZYGOUS AND HETEROZYGOUS

Biologists use some complex terms to describe the alleles in a pair. If the two alleles are the same—CC in the flower color experiment, for example—they form a homozygous (matching) pair. If they are different, such as Cc, then the pair is heterozygous (nonmatching).

plants had purple flowers. That was because the C gene masked the c gene. Biologists call these different forms of the same gene alleles. One allele, C, codes for purple flowers. The other, c, carries the code for white flowers. The C allele is always expressed when present and is referred to as dominant. By contrast, c is expressed only when C is absent and cannot mask its effect (here leading to white-flowered plants). Alleles like c are called recessive.

THE LAW OF SEGREGATION

All the F1 flowers are purple since their genotypes are all Cc. Take a look at the Punnett squares on 12 to see why. The F1 plants have an allele, c, that would lead to white flowers if the dominant C allele were absent. Each sex cell receives just one of the alleles—this is Mendel's first law, the Law of Segregation.

By crossing an F1 plant with itself, young with one of three genotypes are possible; CC, Cc, and cc. The Punnett

sex cell produced by the purple-flowered plant contained one C gene. Each sex cell produced by the white-flowered plant contained a single c gene.

The F1 generation received one gene from each parent. However, all the young

THE ROLE OF CHANCE

The way alleles get to the next generation is mostly random. Whether the pollen grain that fertilizes an egg carries a recessive or a dominant allele is a chance event. Imagine if Mendel had looked at just a couple of heterozygous (Cc) plants in his flower color experiment. A plant would produce roughly equal numbers of pollen grains with c and pollen grains with C.

However, through chance only pollen with c may end up pollinating the other plants. Mendel used thousands of plants in his experiments to minimize the influence of chance on his results.

TEST CROSSING TO DETERMINE GENOTYPE

Mendel realized he could check the genotypes of his plants by test crossing. To find out the genotype of a purple-flowered pea plant, Mendel crossed it with a plant known to have two recessive alleles for flower color. That was easy enough to find out; plants with two recessive alleles had white flowers. Mendel knew that a pea with white flowers must have a cc genotype. He knew the test plant had at least one C because it had purple flowers. If its genotype was CC (1), all the F1 young would be purple-flowered (since they would all be Cc). If the genotype of the plant he was testing was Cc (2), half of the young would have white flowers (since they would be cc).

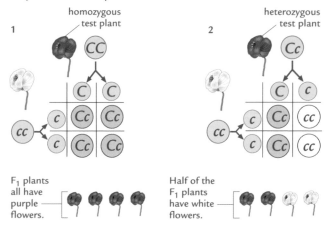

1

homozygous test plant — CC

2

heterozygous test plant — Cc

F_1 plants all have purple flowers.

Half of the F_1 plants have white flowers.

square on page 10 shows why this is so. Three genotypes, but only two possible phenotypes: Since C masks c, CC and Cc produce the same result. Three-quarters of the F2 young have purple flowers; the rest have white ones.

THE LAW OF INDEPENDENT ASSORTMENT

When a plant makes sex cells, do alleles from its mother go into one sex cell and those from its father go into another? Or can a single sex cell contain alleles from both mother and father? Mendel designed an experiment to find out. A diagram showing what happened is on page 16.

Peas have genes for seed color and seed shape. Color has two alleles: Dominant Y, which produces yellow seeds, and y, which is recessive and leads to green seeds. Shape is also controlled by two alleles. Dominant R produces round seeds, while recessive r produces wrinkled seeds.

In Mendel's experiment one parent produced round, yellow seeds (so its genotype was YY RR), and the other produced wrinkled, green seeds (yy rr). A cross between them produced F1 plants that were heterozygous for both genes—in other words, Yy Rr. The F1 plants had dominant alleles; they were yellow and round. Mendel then self-pollinated the F1 plants. If the alleles maintained the associations they had in the parent plants, then the F1 plants would produce sex cells with one of two types of genotypes—YR and yr. Then three-quarters of the F2 plants would have yellow, round seeds, and one-quarter would have green, wrinkled seeds.

THE PRINCIPLE OF DOMINANCE

What makes one allele dominant but another recessive? Genes direct the production of proteins such as enzymes inside cells—that's all they do. A dominant allele produces enzymes that carry out a specific function. Recessive alleles do not code for these enzymes. So dominant alleles get things done; recessive alleles do not.

A single dominant allele must produce enough of the enzyme to produce its associated physical expression, or phenotype. Sometimes, however, that does not occur. A snapdragon plant with red flowers crossed with one with white flowers produces F1 snapdragons with pink flowers. This is caused by something called incomplete dominance.

In the snapdragons a dominant allele (P) produces red pigment. In plants that are heterozygous (Pp) the plant can produce enough pigment to appear pink but no more. To be red, a snapdragon must be homozygous (PP), with pigment produced by a pair of dominant alleles.

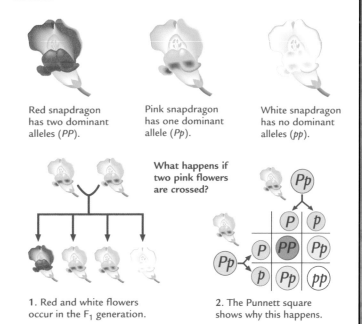

Red snapdragon has two dominant alleles (*PP*).

Pink snapdragon has one dominant allele (*Pp*).

White snapdragon has no dominant alleles (*pp*).

What happens if two pink flowers are crossed?

1. Red and white flowers occur in the F₁ generation.

2. The Punnett square shows why this happens.

INHERITANCE PATTERN FOR PARENTS DIFFERING IN TWO TRAITS

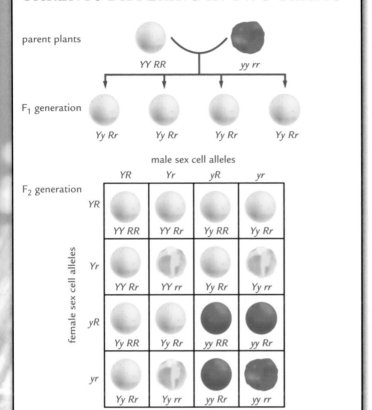

parent plants

YY RR   yy rr

F₁ generation

Yy Rr   Yy Rr   Yy Rr   Yy Rr

male sex cell alleles

F₂ generation

female sex cell alleles

	YR	Yr	yR	yr
YR	YY RR	YY Rr	Yy RR	Yy Rr
Yr	YY Rr	YY rr	Yy Rr	Yy rr
yR	Yy RR	Yy Rr	yy RR	yy Rr
yr	Yy Rr	Yy rr	yy Rr	yy rr

F₂ proportions of color and shape

shape   75% / 25%
color   75% / 25%

overall ratio of the phenotypes

9	3	3	1

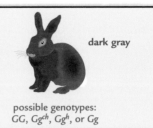

dark gray

possible genotypes:
GG, Gg^{ch}, Gg^h, or Gg

cell formation is independent. The F1 plants produce sex cells with four different genotypes in equal numbers. They are YR, yR, Yr, and yr. The Punnett square shows that there are nine possible combinations of genotypes in the F2 young. The young could have any one of three possible color genotypes (YY, Yy, or yy) and three possible shape genotypes (RR, Rr, or rr).

These combinations of genotypes yield four possible phenotypes. They include some combinations that did not appear in the original parent plants, such as yellow wrinkled seeds. The Punnett square enables us to predict how many of each phenotype appear in the F2 generation.

This experiment helped Mendel form his second law, the Law of Independent Assortment: Alleles of different genes separate independently in the formation

There would be no reason to suppose the traits were under the control of different genes since round seeds would always be yellow and wrinkled ones green.

However, this was not the case. The separation of Y from y and R from r in sex

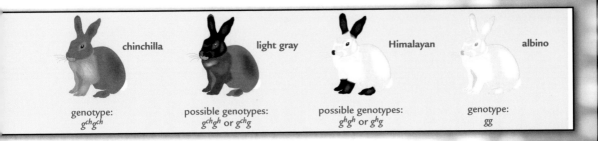

chinchilla
genotype:
$g^{ch}g^{ch}$

light gray
possible genotypes:
$g^{ch}g^h$ or $g^{ch}g$

Himalayan
possible genotypes:
g^hg^h or g^hg

albino
genotype:
gg

THE END OF MENDEL

Mendel later looked at inheritance in plants other than peas. But that just confused matters. For example, hawkweed did not follow the pattern of inheritance Mendel saw in peas. With this setback, plus the minimal impact of his publication on the scientific community and his workload as abbot, Mendel stopped experimenting.

Mendel died in 1884, and the importance of his work remained unrecognized by other scientists until 1903. Although ignored in his lifetime, Mendel is today remembered as the father of genetics and, with Charles Darwin, as one of the greatest biologists in history.

notice. Then other scientists rediscovered Mendel's research and used it to learn more about inheritance. Scientists found that genes occur within chromosomes, and that the genes themselves are formed by stretches of DNA molecules.

In 2003 geneticists completed the Human Genome Project, a map of all the genes of the human body. This incredible achievement could not have taken place without Mendel's work in the abbey gardens almost 150 years ago.

of sex cells. There can be many different alleles for any one gene. For example, rabbit coat color is determined by one gene with four different alleles.

REDISCOVERING MENDEL

Mendel published his work in 1866. For around 40 years no one took much

CHAPTER THREE

THE PROCESS OF CELL DIVISION

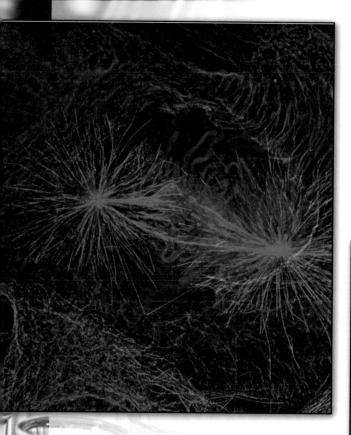

This cell is preparing to divide. The spindle is beginning to form. The chromosomes will line up on the spindle before moving into the new, separate cells.

Growing, healing, and producing young: All these processes depend on the ability of cells to divide.

Cells are the body's building blocks. Every part of your body, from organs like your heart, liver, and stomach to tissues such as nerves and even your blood, contains cells. The function of each cell and how it develops are determined largely by the cell's DNA. DNA carries

PREPARING FOR CELL DIVISION

Cells spend most of their life cycle in interphase. Interphase is a busy time for a cell since it needs to prepare for division. Chemicals that will be needed for the daughter cells are produced. Also, the centrioles copy themselves. They help form the spindle during division. Most importantly, the DNA itself replicates.

That ensures each daughter cell receives a complete set of genetic instructions.

genes, a sequence of instructions telling the cell what to do. You inherited your genes from your parents.

Cells of creatures such as animals and plants contain a control center, or nucleus, that houses the DNA. The nucleus is surrounded by a gel-like cytoplasm within which are various miniorgans, or organelles. All the contents of the cell are wrapped by a plasma membrane.

Cells have life cycles. A typical cell life cycle has two main stages. During the first of them, called interphase, the cell grows and produces proteins and other products. Body cells increase their numbers through a process called mitosis. This is the second stage in the celllife cycle. Cells multiply so dead cells can be replaced and the whole organism can grow. During mitosis a cell divides to produce a pair of new, or daughter, cells. However, each daughter cell needs a complete genome (all the genes in the body) for it to function properly. How do cells manage this feat?

Most cells in your body other than the sex cells contain two complete sets of DNA molecules. One set was provided by your mother, the other by your father. The two

STARTING THE CELL CYCLE

How does a cell know when to perform mitosis? A cell's life cycle is determined by an enzyme inside the nucleus. This enzyme is called cyclin-dependent kinase, or Cdk.

Cdk on its own has no effect on the cell. But when it binds to a protein, cyclin, Cdk's shape is altered. That exposes the "active site" of Cdk; it then triggers the cell to prepare for mitosis.

STRUCTURE OF THE CELL

ribosome (protein production)

rough endoplasmic reticulum

cytoplasm (cell contents)

plasma membrane

smooth endoplasmic reticulum (used for processing proteins)

nucleus (contains DNA)

nuclear envelope

centrioles (used in division)

lysosome (breaks down large molecules)

mitochondrion (place of energy production)

Golgi apparatus (modifies proteins

A typical animal body cell. The various parts inside, such as the mitochondria and nucleus, are called organelles.

GROWTH FACTORS AND HEALING

Cdk provides an internal control for the cell cycle, but mitosis can also be triggered by chemicals from outside the cell. They are called growth factors. When you cut yourself, cell fragments called platelets gather at the wound and help the blood clot. The platelets release a growth factor that drifts into nearby cells, causing them to divide. In this way the wound soon begins to heal.

The body repairs a wound by releasing growth factors.

sets are very similar, but not identical. The DNA is packaged up with proteins in a complex mixture called chromatin. During interphase the chromatin in a body cell remains inside the nucleus, where it is strung out thinly and cannot be seen through a microscope.

THE PROCESS OF MITOSIS

Preparations for cell division are made during interphase. A pair of tiny rods called centrioles begin to replicate (copy themselves). Also, the cell's DNA replicates. This is an essential part of the process, since both of the cells produced by cell division need their own complete set of DNA.

Mitosis begins as the chromatin separates away from other proteins in the nucleus. The chromatin fibers shorten and thicken before coiling into sausage-shaped structures. They are called chromatids. Because the DNA in the cell replicated, there are two identical copies of each chromatid.

CANCER AND THE CELL CYCLE

Study of the cell cycle helps biologists figure out the causes of cancer. Cancer cells divide uncontrollably. They form growths called tumors. Genes controlling cell division may be defective in some cancer cells. Others may produce their own growth factors, leading to continuous cell division.

Identical pairs of chromatids link up to form X-shaped structures called chromosomes. The point in the middle of the X where the two chromatids join is called the centromere.

THE SPINDLE FORMS

Next, the two pairs of centrioles that formed during the cell's interphase move to opposite ends of the cell. A structure that looks like a birdcage forms between the pairs. It is called the spindle. The spindle acts as a kind of railroad track, controlling the way the chromosomes move. Meanwhile, the membrane that surrounds the nucleus, the nuclear envelope, begins to break down.

Mitosis is described in steps 2–5 on this diagram. The distinct stages of mitosis are called prophase, metaphase, anaphase, and telophase.

THE STAGES OF MITOSIS

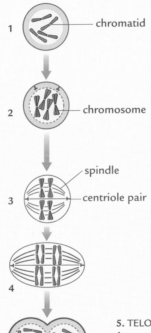

1. **INTERPHASE**
The parent cell prepares for division; DNA and the centrioles replicate.

MITOSIS

2. **PROPHASE**
The chromatids condense and form chromosomes. The nuclear envelope around the nucleus breaks down, and the spindle starts to form.

3. **METAPHASE**
The chromosomes align on the equator of the spindle.

4. **ANAPHASE**
The chromosomes are pulled apart, with chromatids moving to opposite ends of the cell.

5. **TELOPHASE**
A new nuclear envelope forms around the chromatids, which begin to unravel.

6. **CYTOKINESIS**
The cytoplasm divides to leave a pair of daughter cells.

chromatid
chromosome
spindle
centriole pair

PARTS OF A CHROMOSOME

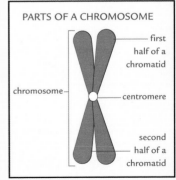

chromosome
first half of a chromatid
centromere
second half of a chromatid

DIVISION OCCURS

The chromosomes begin to coil tighter and tighter. They line up along the equator, which is the middle of the spindle. The chromosomes attach at their centromeres to the spindle fibers. Then the cell and the spindle begin to stretch out. This pulls apart the identical chromatid pairs that form each chromosome. The chromatids move farther and farther along the spindle framework toward the centrioles, which lie at each end of the dividing cell.

The chromatids (or daughter chromosomes, as they are now called) reach the ends of the cell. A new nuclear envelope forms around each set of chromosomes. The chromosomes begin to unravel back into chromatin, and the spindle breaks down. All is now set for the physical division of one cell into two.

Tiny filaments contract at the equator, narrowing the cell. The cell then splits into two halves, or daughter cells. Both of the daughter cells contain a complete set of genes that is identical to that of the original cell.

CELL DIVISION IN PLANTS

Cell division in plants differs from that of animals. Plant cells are encased by rigid cell walls formed by a chemical called cellulose. That means they cannot constrict to divide as animal cells can. Instead, a new cell wall must be built between the daughter nuclei before the new cells can separate. Materials for building the wall are delivered in tiny fluid-filled sacs. The sacs stick together to form a platelike structure. The raw materials are assembled inside this structure into tough cellulose fibers.

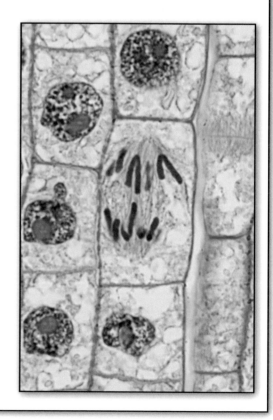

The chromosomes (red) of this onion root cell are lining up on the spindle, ready to separate before the cell divides into two.

THE CREATION OF SEX CELLS

Most of the cells inside your body are diploid. That means they contain two sets of chromosomes, one provided by your mother and the other from your father, with 46 in total. Mitosis leads to the production of two daughter cells, each of which also has 46 chromosomes. But what happens when sex cells such as sperm and eggs fuse at fertilization?

If the sex cells were diploid, the resulting zygote (fertilized egg that develops into young) would have four copies of each chromosome—92 in total. The offspring of such a creature would have 184 chromosomes, and so on. To avoid this, sex cells need to be haploid—they must contain just one set of chromosomes. That ensures the zygote receives just the right number of chromosomes and no more.

Sperm and eggs are formed through a different type of cell division. Biologists call this meiosis. The process of meiosis leads to the formation of haploid cells. For example, human sperm and eggs contain 23 chromosomes rather than the 46 found in the nuclei of other body cells.

MEIOSIS PROMOTES VARIATION

Meiosis differs in another crucial way from mitosis. Mitosis is a mechanism for constancy. It ensures that the same set of genes appears in all the cells in the body. By contrast, meiosis promotes genetic variation. The process leads to differences between the original DNA and that of the resulting sex cells.

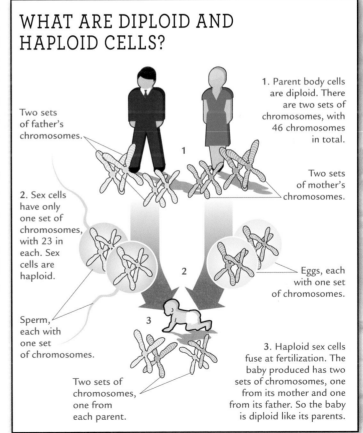

WHAT ARE DIPLOID AND HAPLOID CELLS?

Two sets of father's chromosomes.

1. Parent body cells are diploid. There are two sets of chromosomes, with 46 chromosomes in total.

Two sets of mother's chromosomes.

2. Sex cells have only one set of chromosomes, with 23 in each. Sex cells are haploid.

Eggs, each with one set of chromosomes.

Sperm, each with one set of chromosomes.

Two sets of chromosomes, one from each parent.

3. Haploid sex cells fuse at fertilization. The baby produced has two sets of chromosomes, one from its mother and one from its father. So the baby is diploid like its parents.

WHAT IS A KARYOTYPE?

A karyotype is an organized, visual profile of a person's chromosomes. Chromosomes are arranged and numbered by size, from largest to smallest, with the sex chromosomes last.

To make a karyotype, a physician stains dividing cells to make the chromosomes visible and to add bands on them that match certain gene sequences.

Then the physician takes an image and uses computer software to arrange the chromosomes according to size and banding patterns. That helps the physician quickly identify major chromosome disorders.

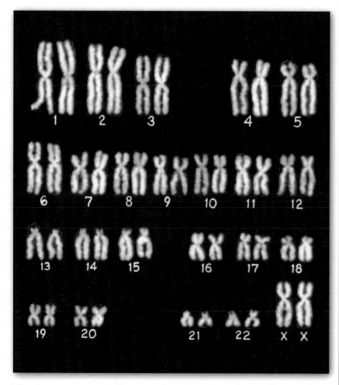

The karyotype of a human female. How do we know the sex of the person?

A little variation between the generations is a good thing for organisms that reproduce sexually, such as humans. Variation can be acted on by natural selection, which helps organisms cope with changes in their environment. The diversity fostered by the process of meiosis explains why you look similar to your parents, brothers, and sisters, but not identical to them.

HOW MEIOSIS WORKS

Meiosis causes cells to divide twice, although the cell's DNA only replicates once. The main objective of the first division is to promote genetic diversity. One-half of the 46 chromosomes inside each of your body cells is provided by your mother, with the other half provided by your father. Each pair of chromosomes is called a homologous pair, meaning they are similar in size and appearance (except the sex chromosomes, which might not match). Each chromosome in a homologous pair carries genes for the same traits, such as eye color. However, each chromosome may carry a different form, or allele, of that gene. One allele may lead to brown eyes, and the other might produce blue eyes.

Before meiosis can take place in your body, the cell must prepare for division. The DNA replicates, as do the centrioles. As in mitosis, the chromatin fibers thicken, and identical pairs join at the centromere to form X-shaped chromosomes. But next the pairs of chromosomes join together to form structures called tetrads. One chromosome in a tetrad consists of two copies of the DNA code contributed by your dad. The other chromosome that makes up the tetrad is similar, but from your mom.

CROSSING OVER

The chromosomes forming the tetrads lie alongside each other. Corresponding genes on each match exactly. At this point the first process that increases genetic diversity takes place. It is called crossing over. Parts

WHEN DOES MEIOSIS TAKE PLACE?

Cells that divide to form sex cells have life cycles like any other cell, although such cycles can last for many years. If you are a girl, oogenesis—the process of egg formation—began before you were born. However, completion of meiosis is delayed until puberty, around age 13. From then on, meiosis continues, with one egg completing its development each month until you reach age 50 or thereabouts. If you are a boy, the production of sperm, or spermatogenesis, will not begin until you are around 14. The process will then continue for the rest of your life.

Meiosis is occurring inside these teenagers. The boys are producing sperm, while one egg inside each girl completes its development each month.

THE STAGES OF MEIOSIS

1. PROPHASE I
Chromatids join to form chromosomes. Matching pairs of chromosomes link up to form tetrads, and may occur. The nuclear envelope breaks down, and the spindle forms.

CROSSING OVER

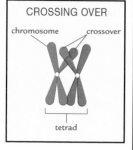

chromosome

crossover

tetrad

2. METAPHASE I
The tetrads line up randomly on the spindle.

spindle

3. ANAPHASE I
The tetrads move to opposite ends of the cell.

4. TELOPHASE I
The chromosomes unravel, and nuclear envelopes re-form; the cells then physically divide.

5. PROPHASE II
The nuclear envelopes break down, and spindles begin to re-form.

6. METAPHASE II
The chromosomes line up along the spindle equator.

7. ANAPHASE II
The chromatids that form each chromosome are pulled apart.

8. TELOPHASE II
Nuclear envelopes re-form, and cells narrow at their equators.

9. CYTOKINESIS
The cells divide, leaving four haploid sex cells.

of each chromosome within a tetrad break at corresponding points, and chunks of DNA are swapped. This random process mixes the DNA you inherited from your mother and father.

Meanwhile, the nuclear envelope dissolves away, and a spindle forms that pushes the centriole pairs to opposite ends of the cell. The tetrads attach to the spindle and move to the equator. The way they line up there is random. Chromosomes provided by your mother or father may be on either side. The tetrads split, and the chromosomes are pulled to opposite ends of the cell. The cell then splits as in mitosis to leave a pair of daughter cells. The random way the tetrads align is the second source of genetic diversity; chromosomes from your mom or dad could end up in either daughter cell.

There are two cell divisions in meiosis, each with a set of stages. The name of each stage is followed by a number that explains which of the divisions is taking place.

PRODUCING EGGS AND SPERM

Through crossover and the random alignment of tetrads on the spindle the daughter cells' DNA differs from the original DNA. Now the daughter cells divide again to form sex cells. This time the DNA does not replicate. The division process is similar to mitosis. Chromosomes align on a spindle before being pulled to opposite ends of each cell, which then divides.

When meiosis is complete, the one original cell has produced four sex cells. Each of these cells contains just one set of chromosomes—in other words, the cells are haploid. Each can now fuse with a sex cell from a mate to form a zygote.

ERRORS IN MEIOSIS

Sometimes meiosis goes wrong. For example, if chromosome pair 21 fails to separate from the tetrad, both may go to the same end of one of the daughter cells. The resulting eggs will have either two or no copies of this chromosome. Imagine that an egg with two copies of this chromosome is fertilized by a normal sperm. The zygote that forms has three copies of the chromosome. A child born with this extra copy is said to have Down syndrome.

POLYPLOID ORGANISMS

Most plants and animals, such as humans, are diploid. Their genetic material includes two chromosome sets. Sometimes, however, offspring inherit more than two sets of chromosomes due to mistakes in meiosis. That is usually deadly for animals, but some plants can cope. Plants with extra chromosome sets are called polyploids. Many crop plants are polyploids. Sometimes the extra set comes from the same species. Bananas, for example, have three chromosome sets. That leads to large, seedless fruit. Bananas are sterile (cannot reproduce), though. New plants can only grow from cuttings.

Some other crops contain extra sets of chromosomes from different species. Wheat has six chromosome sets. That is because wheat descends from three different ancestors, each of which contributed two sets of chromosomes.

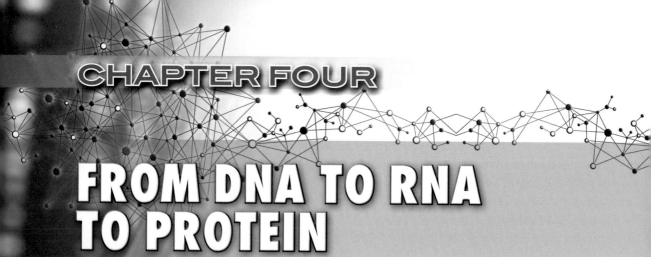

CHAPTER FOUR

FROM DNA TO RNA TO PROTEIN

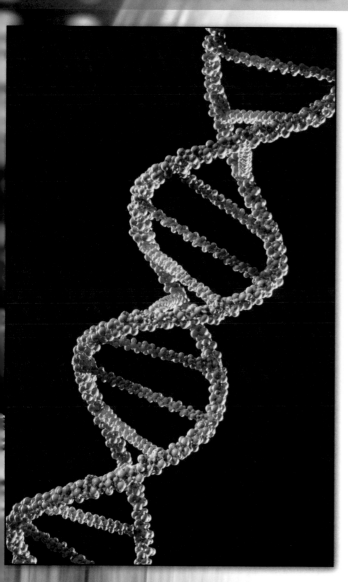

The genetic material inside the cells of almost all living organisms is made of a chemical called DNA. A similar chemical, RNA, is important for producing proteins.

Chemistry plays a crucial role in genetics, the study of inheritance. Gregor Mendel (1822–1884) figured out the ways that certain characteristics passed from parents to young. Mendel suggested that "particles" were somehow involved. However, the chemical nature of these particles—now called genes—was not identified for another 90 years. The key chemical in inheritance is called deoxyribonucleic acid, or DNA for short.

COMPONENTS OF DNA

A DNA molecule is shaped like a ladder that has been twisted around itself many times without breaking the rungs. This

The structure of DNA, the chemical that lies at the heart of inheritance.

shape is called a double helix. The building blocks of DNA are called nucleotides. They are made of chemicals called phosphates as well as sugars. The sugars and phosphates form the "sides" of the DNA ladder.

Nucleotides also contain one of four other chemicals called bases. They are adenine (A), thymine (T), guanine (G), and cytosine (C). The bases form the ladder's "rungs." Bases on one side of the DNA ladder bind with bases on the other in a very specific way. Adenine in one strand always forms a bond to thymine in the other, while guanine always bonds with cytosine.

WHAT DOES DNA DO?

In organisms such as animals and plants DNA occurs in the nuclei (control centers) of cells. DNA carries genes, which are sets of instructions formed by the order of the bases on the DNA molecule.

TYPES OF DNA

Although the double helix shape is famous and familiar, it is not the only structure that DNA can occur as inside living organisms. Some viruses have DNA with just a single strand. The ends of this strand may join to form a ring. Other viruses and all other organisms have double-stranded DNA. However, sometimes the ends of the strands join together, or the molecule may be ring-shaped. Some organisms even have "supercoiled" DNA that is twisted in on itself many more times than usual.

Genes direct the production of a range of vital chemicals called proteins. There can be thousands of genes on any one DNA molecule, and each gene directs the production of a different protein. Some proteins help form structures like tissues and organs. Others form cell products such as hormones.

BASE PAIRING IN A DNA MOLECULE

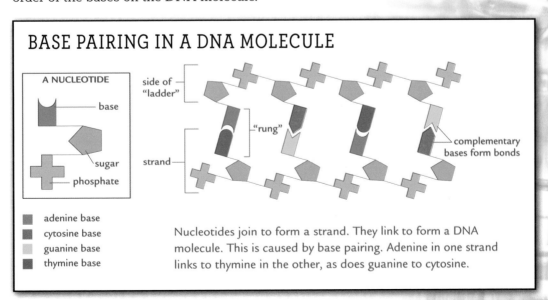

A NUCLEOTIDE
- base
- sugar
- phosphate

side of "ladder"
strand
"rung"
complementary bases form bonds

- adenine base
- cytosine base
- guanine base
- thymine base

Nucleotides join to form a strand. They link to form a DNA molecule. This is caused by base pairing. Adenine in one strand links to thymine in the other, as does guanine to cytosine.

EXTRACT DNA FROM FRUIT

To take a look at some DNA, try this fun experiment. You will need a bowl of ice, a bottle of methylated spirits (or rubbing alcohol), a kiwi fruit, a knife, 2 measuring cups, kitchen scales, some salt, a measuring cylinder, water, dishwashing liquid, a strainer or cheesecloth, a large spoon, a tall glass, and some wire.

1. Put the bottle of spirits (or rubbing alcohol) on the ice—they must be very cold. These liquids are dangerous, so ask an adult to help. Then peel and chop the kiwi fruit, and put the pieces into a measuring cup.

2. Stir together 1/10 ounce (3g) of salt, 1/3 fluid ounce (10ml) of dishwashing liquid, and 3 fluid ounces (100ml) of water.

3. Add the dishwashing liquid–salt solution to the fruit in the measuring cup. Mash it up, then let it sit for 15 minutes.

4. Hold the strainer over the glass, and pour the green mush through, catching the liquid in the glass. You will need to fill about one-fifth of the glass with the liquid.

6. You should see a white layer form in between the layers of green and purple liquids. Congratulations! You have successfully isolated the kiwi fruit's DNA. Fish out the DNA by winding it carefully onto the wire for a closer look.

5

5. Very carefully drizzle the ice-cold methylated spirits on the back of the spoon so that it forms a purple layer on top of the green liquid. Stop when the glass is about two-fifths full. Set the glass on the table, and watch what happens.

4

2

6

HOW LONG IS DNA?

The DNA of a single *Escherichia coli* bacterium is about 4 million base pairs long. Stretched out flat, this DNA measures around 0.05 inches (1.4 mm) long—much longer than the bacterium itself. The DNA forms a ring that is squashed up small to fit inside the bacterial cell. This arrangement doesn't work for creatures with longer DNA molecules, such as humans, though. DNA in these organisms is wound tightly with proteins to form a material called chromatin. Human DNA contains around 3 billion bases. Using the figures for *E. coli* DNA, can you estimate how long DNA from a single human cell would be if it were laid out flat?

If the DNA from every cell in a person's body were laid end to end, the DNA would reach to the sun and back more than 3,000 times!

Among the most important proteins are enzymes. They control the rate at which chemical reactions take place inside the body. Thousands of different chemical reactions occur inside a body cell. Some help make new cell products or parts; others are important for releasing energy or in cell division. None of these essential reactions could take place without the help of enzymes.

Proteins such as enzymes determine everything about an organism, from what it looks like to how its body parts function. That is why DNA is such an important molecule; without DNA proteins could not be made.

DNA REPLICATION

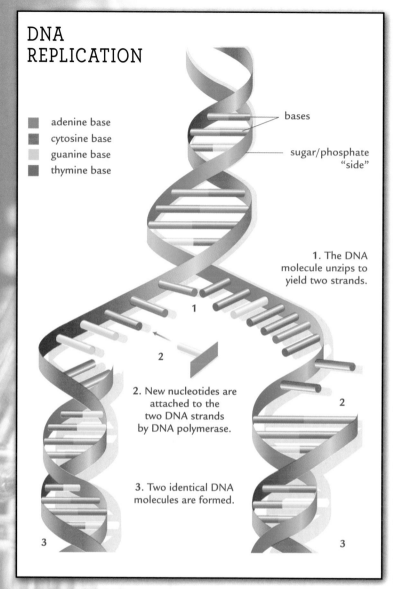

- adenine base
- cytosine base
- guanine base
- thymine base

bases

sugar/phosphate "side"

1. The DNA molecule unzips to yield two strands.

2. New nucleotides are attached to the two DNA strands by DNA polymerase.

3. Two identical DNA molecules are formed.

DNA replication ensures that cells formed by division contain a set of genes identical to that of the parent cell.

divide so the organism can grow and repair itself. But each new cell needs a complete set of genes to allow it to function properly. To ensure that happens, DNA molecules inside a cell that is about to divide go through a process of self-copying, or replication.

Replication produces an exact copy of the DNA of the dividing cell. The first step in replication involves the uncoiling of the double helix. Each double helix "ladder" then separates to form two strands. The paired bases that make up the "rungs" separate, and the two "sides" of the ladder unzip. Each strand will form a template for a new DNA double helix.

For the next step in the replication process an enzyme called DNA polymerase is needed. This enzyme helps nucleotides that are loose in the cell join to the

HOW DNA REPLICATES

With the exception of viruses, the process of cell division is essential for living creatures. Bacteria divide to produce more bacteria; cells inside animals and plants strands. Molecules of adenine link to thymine, and molecules of guanine bond to cytosine. The DNA polymerase moves along the template DNA strand, attaching the correct nucleotides as it goes.

The end result is two DNA molecules that are identical to the original version. Each consists of one new strand and one old one. The cell can now divide to produce two cells, each with a full complement of DNA.

DNA replication is essential for the growth of an organism and also for the inheritance of characteristics. Replication allows the genes of an individual to be carried in their sperm or eggs and passed on to the next generation.

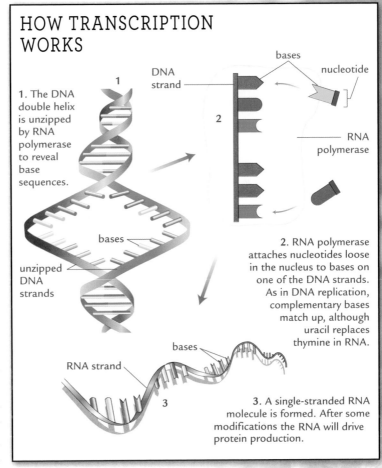

HOW TRANSCRIPTION WORKS

1. The DNA double helix is unzipped by RNA polymerase to reveal base sequences.

DNA strand

bases

nucleotide

2

RNA polymerase

bases

unzipped DNA strands

2. RNA polymerase attaches nucleotides loose in the nucleus to bases on one of the DNA strands. As in DNA replication, complementary bases match up, although uracil replaces thymine in RNA.

bases

RNA strand

3

3. A single-stranded RNA molecule is formed. After some modifications the RNA will drive protein production.

In transcription the base code on the DNA is used to make RNA. The RNA later moves from the nucleus to a ribosome, where it determines which proteins are made by the cell.

TRANSCRIPTION

Once a pair of new cells has formed following cell division (see 17–20), they get to work making proteins according to the instructions provided by the DNA. How does the DNA's sequence of bases control this process? To make proteins, another molecule, ribonucleic acid or

RNA, is needed. Like DNA, RNA is made up of nucleotides. The two chemicals are similar, although RNA is smaller and occurs as a single strand rather than as a double helix.

RNA takes the code from DNA to the parts of the cell where proteins are made;

REPAIRING ERRORS

DNA replicates with astonishing accuracy. Scientists have estimated that an error occurs in a gene only once in about one million cell divisions. How is the process so reliable? Many errors are removed by natural selection; the cell dies before it can divide. Other mistakes are corrected. A system of enzymes inside each cell scans DNA molecules after they have replicated. The enzymes then fix any mistakes in the base sequence.

Part of the rough endoplasmic reticulum (ER), a network of folded membranes that occur in a cell's cytoplasm. The little granules on the surface of the ER are ribosomes, where protein production occurs.

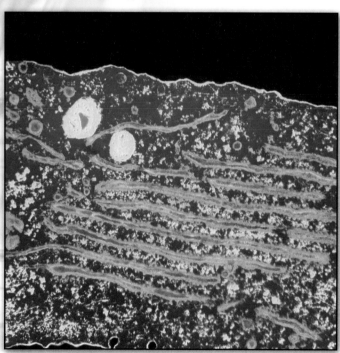

it acts as an information carrier. RNA itself is made in a process called transcription. First, an enzyme called RNA polymerase unzips part of the DNA double helix. That makes certain sequences of bases—the genes—accessible. One of the strands acts as a template in a way similar to DNA replication. The RNA polymerase moves along the strand, joining complementary nucleotides. This produces a strand of RNA. The RNA bears a sequence of nucleotides identical to that of the DNA strand that did not act as the template. The only difference is that thymine is replaced in RNA by a fifth type of base, uracil (U). Uracil binds only to adenine, as thymine does.

More enzymes swiftly go to work on the new RNA strand, sometimes even before transcription is complete. The enzymes add a sequence of bases at the end called the tail and a single base at the front called the cap. The tail and cap sequences protect the important parts of the RNA molecule from damage. Segments of the code called introns that play no part in protein production are removed. The finished product is called messenger RNA, or mRNA.

TRANSLATION

Next, the sequence of bases on the mRNA molecule is used to make proteins. This

THE TRIPLET CODE

There are 20 amino acids that, in different combinations, form the thousands of different proteins inside an organism. Each amino acid is coded for by a group of three bases on the DNA molecule. These bases correspond to another set of three bases—called a triplet—on the mRNA. Because there are four possible bases (A, G, C, and U), there are 64 (4 x 4 x 4) possible combinations of bases in a triplet. As a result, several different triplets can code for any one amino acid.

Triplets are also involved in starting and stopping translation, the process of protein production using the RNA template. The triplet AUG, which codes for

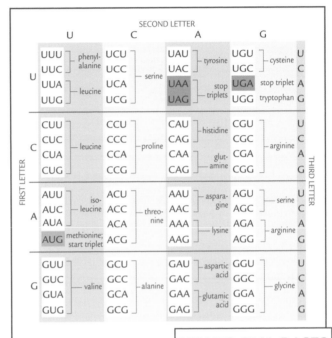

SECOND LETTER

KEY TO RNA BASES

| U | uracil | C | cytosine |
| A | adenine | G | guanine |

the amino acid methionine, serves as a startup code for translation. Other amino acids are then joined to form the protein. Eventually, one of three "stop" triplets is reached. They are UAA, UAG, and UGA. This brings translation to a halt. The finished protein product is now ready for use.

process is called translation. The mRNA drifts from the nucleus into the cytoplasm (the part of the cell that lies outside the nucleus). There the mRNA's cap binds to a tiny organelle (miniorgan) called a ribosome. This is where the production of proteins takes place.

Biologists refer to the order of bases on the mRNA molecule as the triplet code.

It is called that because a set of three bases (or triplet) codes for one type of amino acid (see box on 33). There are 20 different amino acids that occur in

WHAT IS A GENE?

You have probably heard the word "gene" again and again, but what exactly is a gene? A gene is a segment of DNA that serves as a template for a certain protein. A gene includes a promoter, a sequence of bases that regulates the process of transcription to make RNA. A series of bases then determines the order of the RNA bases, which in turn codes for the amino acids in the protein produced by the gene. The final base sequence (often AATAAA) brings transcription to a halt.

organisms; they are the building blocks of proteins. The triplet code determines which amino acids join together where.

INTRONS AND EXONS

The base sequences of animal and plant DNA that code for proteins occur in blocks called exons. Between the exons are sections that do not code for proteins. They are called introns. Introns must be removed before the mRNA moves from the nucleus to the ribosome to make proteins. Some introns remove themselves from the mRNA; for most, though, enzymes are needed to snip them free. Things are simpler in the DNA of bacteria; they have no introns present that need to be removed.

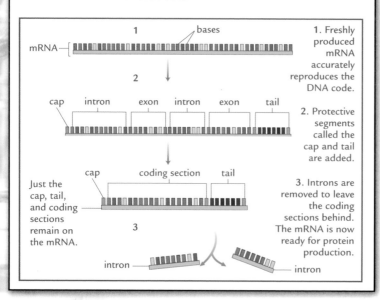

1. Freshly produced mRNA accurately reproduces the DNA code.

2. Protective segments called the cap and tail are added.

3. Introns are removed to leave the coding sections behind. The mRNA is now ready for protein production.

Meanwhile, different RNA molecules called transfer RNA (tRNA) bind to amino acids that are loose in the cell. Each tRNA molecule is formed by three nucleotides. The sequence of bases on the tRNA determines which type of amino acid it can join to.

FINAL STEPS

Complete with its amino acid luggage, a tRNA molecule with the correct sequence of nucleotides binds to an mRNA triplet. The ribosome holds the two RNA molecules in place. Another tRNA molecule plus amino acid then attaches to the next mRNA triplet along. That brings the two amino acids into close contact. The ribosome joins the amino

HOW PROTEINS ARE MADE

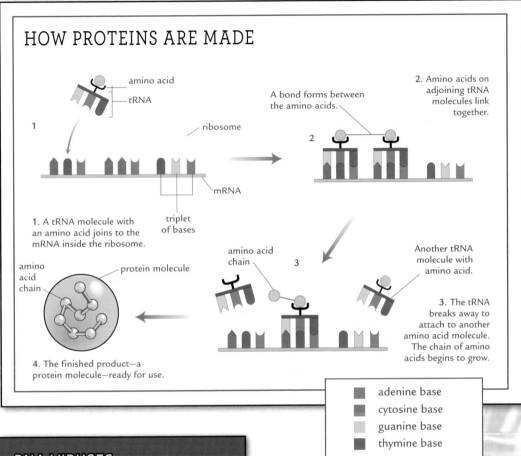

amino acid

tRNA

1

ribosome

mRNA

1. A tRNA molecule with an amino acid joins to the mRNA inside the ribosome.

triplet of bases

A bond forms between the amino acids.

2. Amino acids on adjoining tRNA molecules link together.

2

amino acid chain

3

Another tRNA molecule with amino acid.

3. The tRNA breaks away to attach to another amino acid molecule. The chain of amino acids begins to grow.

amino acid chain

protein molecule

4. The finished product—a protein molecule—ready for use.

adenine base
cytosine base
guanine base
thymine base

RNA VIRUSES

DNA forms the genetic material of most types of organisms—but not all. In some viruses, such as HIV and the virus that causes the illness hepatitis C, RNA replaces DNA to serve as the organism's genetic code.

The ribosome moves along the mRNA strand, repeating the process as it goes. The new protein molecule is now starting to take shape.

The chain of amino acids grows longer and longer. Eventually, the protein molecule is finished. It contains a sequence of amino acids that was determined by the triplets on the mRNA strand. They, in turn, were determined by the makeup of the DNA molecule back in the nucleus.

acids together before breaking the first tRNA free. The tRNA then floats away to bond with another amino acid.

A STRUCTURAL STORY

Despite previous breakthroughs, it was not until 1953 that scientists fully understood the essential role of DNA. In that year English scientists James Watson (born 1928) and Francis Crick (born 1916) proposed that the DNA molecule formed a double helix shape. They based their work on the research of Czech biochemist Erwin Chargaff (1905–2002), who figured out that bases in DNA match to form pairs. However, critical evidence for their theory was provided by fellow English scientists Maurice Wilkins (born 1916) and Rosalind Franklin (1920–1958). They used X-rays to show that DNA formed a helix.

These branches of evidence allowed Watson and Crick to build a model of the DNA molecule. Their research proved that the base sequence provided more than enough information to account for the complexities of protein production. The revelation of the structure of DNA was arguably the most important biological discovery of the 20th century.

Crick (*right*) and Watson display their DNA model in 1953.

AMPLIFYING DNA

DNA breaks down into tiny pieces soon after death to find DNA in fossil remains is an exceptionally rare occurrence. Even when DNA is present, it is fragmented. However, just a single fragment can be amplified so it can be studied. The technique scientists use to do this is called the polymerase chain reaction, or PCR. The strands of the sample DNA are separated by heating. Then tiny pieces of DNA made by the scientists called primers are added. They attach to the sample DNA, and an enzyme, polymerase, is added. The enzyme allows new strands to form that are identical to the regions around the primers. Repeating the sequence again and again increases the sample DNA until enough is present for analysis. Using PCR, DNA samples have been analyzed from the bones of Neanderthal people and mammoths. DNA from even older fossils, such as that of a 20-million-year-old magnolia leaf, has also been sampled.

The newly formed protein folds in a certain way before drifting off to carry out whatever function it is required for.

GENE REGULATION

Although DNA molecules must replicate in their entirety before a cell divides, genes are not active in all of the cells all of the time. Any cell only has a limited number of functions in the body.

For example, pituitary cells produce hormones that are not produced by any other body cells. There is control over which genes become active in any one cell and when. Regulator proteins are responsible for this control. They are enzymes that bind to the DNA a little way along from a target gene.

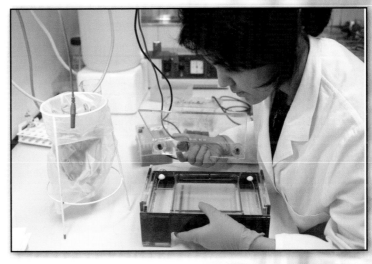

Biologists study DNA using a process called gel electrophoresis. Electricity moves the DNA fragments in a sample, causing them to separate. This leads to distinct bands on the gel that can be stained for study.

Depending on the enzyme, they can either help or hinder the transcription of the gene. That allows genes to be switched on or off.

CHAPTER FIVE

UNDERSTANDING GENOMES

A genome is the complete set of genes an organism has. Biologists have decoded the genomes of several types of organisms.

With the exception of some viruses the inherited material of all organisms is composed of molecules of deoxyribonucleic acid, or DNA. A single molecule of DNA carries units called

HOW BIG IS A GENOME?

The amount of DNA in the nucleus varies enormously between species. As you might expect, multicellular creatures like animals and plants generally have more DNA than single-celled organisms. However, some single-celled creatures, such as amebas, have truly massive genomes. That is

because these creatures are polyploids. This means that at some stage in their evolutionary history they have incorporated the genome of another species into their own.

Research on genome size has revealed some intriguing relationships. For example, genome size corresponds to the size of red blood cells in mammals, despite the fact that mammals' red blood cells contain no DNA. Lungfish and lilies have the largest genomes, at almost 40 times larger than that of a human. Land snail genomes are larger than those of water snails, while flightless birds such as ostriches have larger genomes than their flying relatives.

genes that direct how the cell functions. Genes do this by controlling the production of proteins such as enzymes by the cell. The complete set of genetic material of an organism is called its genome.

The genome of a plant or animal may contain thousands of genes. DNA of these organisms occurs mainly in cell nuclei (control centers). Individuals of any one species have the same number of DNA molecules in each body cell's

The genome of this frog is many times smaller than that of the lily inside which it hides. Why is this?

WHY DO GENOME SIZES VARY?

Why do the genomes of different organisms vary so much in size? Much of the difference is due to the presence of long stretches of noncoding, or junk, DNA. Junk DNA does not have any obvious function. The graph shows how the percentage of useful DNA in a genome drops dramatically with overall genome size. Bacteria do not have any junk DNA, but much of the genomes of more complex organisms is junk. The biggest genomes are 80,000 times larger than those of bacteria. But strip away the junk DNA, and there is only a twenty-fold difference.

WHAT ARE LINKED GENES?

Some genes are said to be linked to others. Genes that lie on the same chromosome are considered linked, even though they code for different features.

The genomes of plants and animals contain many such pairs.

The genes for eye color and body color in fruit flies, for example, are linked. Linked genes may pass from parent to young together, unlike genes that lie on separate chromosomes. The closer together on a chromosome the genes lie, the more closely they are linked, and the likelier it is that they will be passed on together. Linked genes provide a good way to map genes positions on a chromosome.

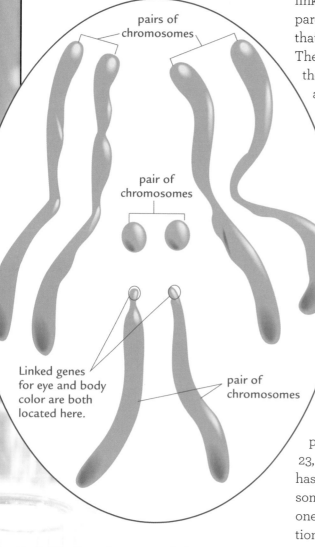

pairs of chromosomes

pair of chromosomes

Linked genes for eye and body color are both located here.

pair of chromosomes

Fruit flies have four pairs of chromosomes. Genes for different traits that occur on any one chromosome are linked.

nucleus. Human body cells contain 46 DNA molecules. Before a cell divides these molecules copy themselves. They then coil to form structures called chromosomes.

The entire set of chromosomes is called the karyotype. Scientists number the pairs of chromosomes within the karyotype in order of size. In people the longest is pair 1, while pair 22 is the shortest. Pair 23, the sex chromosomes, is different. It has at least one very large (X) chromosome and may have one very small (Y) one. Each DNA molecule has a combination of genes along its length that does not change from one individual to the next. So, for example, the gene that codes for the hormone insulin in people always

LEARN ABOUT VARIATION

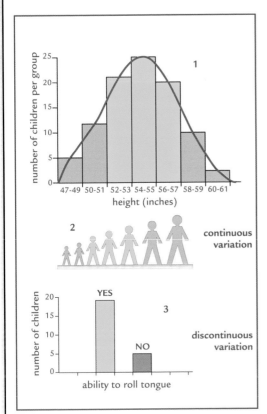

No two people are exactly the same—even identical twins differ in some ways. There are two types of variation, continuous and discontinuous.

Take measurements of the height of children in your school (make sure they are of roughly the same age), and round up or down to the nearest inch. Then plot a graph with 2-inch (5-cm) groups along the bottom and the number of children for each group going upward. Your graph should look something like 1. There is a smooth change from short to tall pupils (2). This is called a continuous variation.

The shape of the graph (the red line) is called a normal distribution. Measure other features, such as weight or arm length, and draw another graph. Are these features normally distributed? Or is the graph skewed (slanted to one side)? Variation is not always continuous.

The ability to roll the tongue into a loop is discontinuous—you can either do it, or you can't (3). Another discontinuous feature is blood type, based on proteins on the surface of red blood cells. People can have either A, B, AB, or O blood type, but nothing else.

occurs close to one end of chromosome 11. The position a gene occupies on a chromosome is called its locus (plural: loci).

INTERACTIONS AMONG GENES

The relationship between a gene and the characteristic it leads to is rarely simple. Some features are influenced by dozens of different genes. Often these characteristics do not follow simple patterns of inheritance. Height in people, for example, involves the interaction of many genes, as well as environmental factors. Some people are tall, others are short, while most are of average height. By contrast, there are only four blood groups—A, B, AB, and O.

TORTOISESHELL AND CALICO CATS

Can you find a male tortoiseshell or calico cat? You might have some problems. A gene on a cat's X chromosome determines the tortoiseshell coat, which is characterized by black and orange markings. A calico cat has white patches as well. Two different alleles are involved. They are "black" and "orange." Tortoiseshell and calico cats have both alleles, which means they must have two X chromosomes. That means they must be female. Male cats have only one X chromosome, so in most cases they cannot be tortoiseshell.

Height is an example of continuous variation, with a large number of possibilities. Blood group is a type of discontinuous variation—a person can have only one of a fixed number of blood types.

Many genes control the function of others. They direct the production of enzymes that regulate the activities of other genes. The enzymes do so by clamping to key positions on the genome. In this way certain genes can stop others from working or switch them on.

A UNIQUE INDIVIDUAL

The genome consists of the gene sequences that occur at precisely defined loci on the chromosomes. But there may be one of several versions of each gene. These variants are called alleles. Alleles explain why you do not look identical to your friends or family. Humans have a variety of eye colors, for example, because there are several eye color alleles. Some combinations lead to blue eyes; others lead to brown, green, or gray.

The combination of alleles in an individual is called the genotype. Every cell inside you carries the same combinations of alleles—they all share the same genotype. That is because each body cell is the product of countless numbers of cell divisions starting from the fertilized egg in your mother's uterus. Each time a cell divides, the DNA inside replicates, keeping the genotype the same in every cell. The precise nature of your genotype depends on the alleles carried by the sperm and the egg that fused to make you.

SETS OF CHROMOSOMES

Matching chromosomes have genes that code for the same features at exactly the same loci. So, for example, there are two copies of the insulin gene in each human body cell because there are two copies of chromosome number 11.

For most animals body cells, such as those of the liver, skin, or heart, carry these double chromosome sets. Cells like these are called diploid. When eggs or sperm form during the process of cell division called meiosis, these sets separate into different daughter cells. Sperm and eggs carry a single copy of each of

DNA HYBRIDIZATION

Similarities between the genomes of different species indicate how closely they are related. To find out how similar two species are, scientists use a technique called DNA hybridization. DNA is isolated from cells of the two organisms and treated with chemicals to separate the strands. The DNA is then mixed together. A strand from one sample tries to reform into a complete DNA molecule with a strand from the other sample. The greater the similarities of the base sequences of the two species, the more successful the pairing up is. DNA strands from closely related species form more new molecules than strands from more distantly related creatures.

This is a red panda. Biologists have used DNA hybridization techniques to show that despite many physical similarities, the red panda is not a close relative of the giant panda. It is actually more closely related to raccoons.

THE SOCIAL LIFE OF ANTS

Ants are social insects that live in colonies. All the young are produced by one ant, the queen, which mated with a male before founding the nest. The worker ants do not lay eggs, but still manage to get their genes into the next generation. How do they manage this?

All depends on the unusual nature of ant genetics. Queen and worker ants are diploid, with two sets of chromosomes. Males, however, are haploid—they only have one chromosome set. As with humans and other diploids, the queen shares half her genes with her young. But each daughter—worker or new queen—shares, on average, three-quarters of her genes with the other daughters. So bizarrely, more of a worker ant's genes pass to the next generation if she does not breed. Instead, it pays for a worker to tend to the queen and help her produce more of the worker's sisters.

In a worker ant's ideal world, all the young produced would be new queens. But the queen needs workers to feed and look after her and the young. So she releases chemicals that control whether a young female ant becomes a queen or a worker. That keeps the numbers of each at the right level.

the chromosomes: These cells are called haploid cells. When sperm fertilizes an egg, the resulting cell (or zygote) has two chromosome sets—it is diploid, just like the body cells of the animal into which the zygote develops.

Not all organisms are diploid. In an ant colony, for example, female worker ants and the queen ant are diploid, but the males are haploid. Many types of plants, as well as some other organisms, have more than two sets of chromosomes in their cells. These creatures are called polyploids.

DECODING GENOMES

Since the 1980s biologists have begun to decode the entire genomes of a number of different organisms. It is hoped that such genome projects will have major effects in medicine, in the

A worker ant tends to the queen. The queen lays all the colony's eggs. Because of ants' unusual genetics more of the worker's genes pass to the next generation than if the worker herself were to breed.

treatment of genetic disorders such as cystic fibrosis.

Early successes involved the decoding of the genomes of fruit flies and roundworms. Later, the human genome was successfully decoded. Other successful projects in recent years have included deciphering the genomes of animals such as dogs, cows, and mice.

STUDYING BACTERIAL GENOMES

As you might expect, the genomes of tiny bacteria are very much smaller than those of multicellular organisms such as animals, plants, and fungi.

THE BOOK OF LIFE

The human genome is more then 3 billion bases long. Imagine an encyclopedia that contained the complete base sequence written out in full, with 3,000 letters per page. The total size of the finished encyclopedia would be 1.3 million pages long—or more than 1,300 volumes at 1,000 pages per volume!

For example, the genome of humans contains nearly 21,000 genes. A group of bacteria called mycoplasmas have the smallest of all known genomes. Their genome contains just 470 genes. With so few genes the mycoplasma genome must

MAPPING GENOMES

Biologists began to decode the entire genomes of animals in the 1980s. Early research programs looked at the genomes of bacteria and other tiny creatures. Later, larger organisms such as fruit flies and roundworms were studied. The greatest achievement in this field to date was the completion of the Human Genome Project (HGP) in 2003. The HGP may lead to dramatic advances in our understanding of various diseases. Since the completion of the project the genomes of other animals have been assembled.

The locations of some genes (with chromosome number) that cause diseases mapped by the HGP.

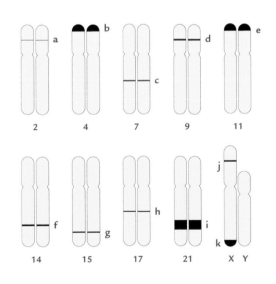

a colon cancer
b Huntington's disease
c cystic fibrosis
d skin cancer
e sickle-cell anemia
f Alzheimer's disease
g Tay-Sachs disease
h breast cancer
i Lou Gehrig's disease
j Duchenne muscular dystrophy
k hemophilia

DECIPHERING DOG DNA

Since the completion of the HGP biologists have begun to unravel the genomes of other mammal species.

In December 2005, an international team of researchers announced the completion of the genome sequence of the dog. The researchers first sequenced the DNA of Tasha, a female boxer (right). They assembled 99 percent of the dog genome.

This and other research will help biologists learn more about the 400 known dog genetic diseases. Many of these disorders have human equivalents. Narcolepsy, for example, is a disorder that causes uncontrollable bursts of sleep in people—and in dogs, too.

GENE PROBES

Scientists can discover the location of a gene in a DNA sample by using a gene probe. A gene probe is a short length of DNA that contains radioactive elements. It releases radioactivity so researchers can pinpoint its location. The gene probe has a series of bases that bond with those of the target gene. To use a gene probe, the strands of the sample DNA molecules are separated. The gene probe is added to the sample. Because their bases are complementary, the radioactive DNA attaches to the target gene. The gene can then be located by detecting the radioactivity.

approach the bare minimum required for cellular (nonvirus) life to exist.

Using mycoplasmas, biologists have learned more about this lower limit in genome size. They have found that there are 337 genes that are essential for life. These genes are universal and occur

SWITCHING ON BACTERIAL GENES

Genes are usually switched on and off by other genes. However, other things can sometimes trigger a gene into action. When some bacteria are exposed to a type of sugar, a gene is switched on that allows them to use the food source. This gene is usually kept switched off by the presence of a chemical. The sugar binds to the chemical, stopping it from blocking the gene. That switches the gene on.

in all cellular organisms. This discovery may lead to the creation of artificial life forms. Scientists could take the key genes and add genes for features such as tolerance of radioactivity. Such bacteria could then be used to clean up spills of nuclear waste.

Artificial bacteria may be made soon. As early as 2003 artificial viruses had already been created. Starting from scratch, scientists used DNA to make an artificial version of an existing type of virus.

This experiment shows how researchers discovered that life's minimum genome contains just 337 genes. By mutating (changing) each gene in turn, the scientists could figure out which were essential for cellular life.

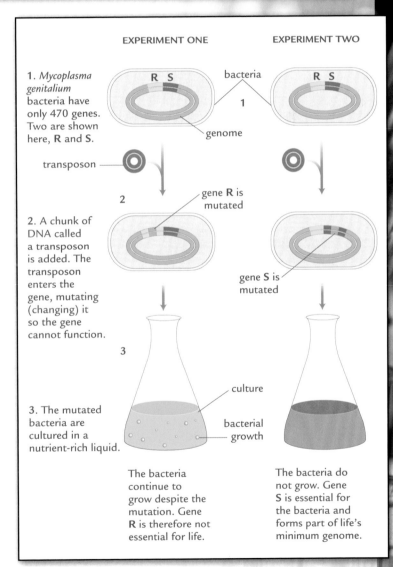

EXPERIMENT ONE   EXPERIMENT TWO

1. *Mycoplasma genitalium* bacteria have only 470 genes. Two are shown here, R and S.

transposon

2. A chunk of DNA called a transposon is added. The transposon enters the gene, mutating (changing) it so the gene cannot function.

gene R is mutated

gene S is mutated

3. The mutated bacteria are cultured in a nutrient-rich liquid.

culture

bacterial growth

The bacteria continue to grow despite the mutation. Gene R is therefore not essential for life.

The bacteria do not grow. Gene S is essential for the bacteria and forms part of life's minimum genome.

WHY DO PEOPLE HAVE JUST TWO SEXES?

Why do people and almost all other organisms have just two sexes? This means that only 50 percent of all the people we meet could potentially be mates. Things are different for some other creatures. Mushrooms have 36,000 sexes, so practically any other mushroom is a potential partner. Why do we not have vast numbers of sexes, too? The answer lies in mtDNA, which replicates and mutates very quickly. Imagine if people had 36,000 sexes. Any mtDNA mutation would spread quickly through the population—a bad mutation would be disastrous. So organisms evolved to have just two sexes, with mitochondria passed on only by females. That means it is trickier to find a mate, but this is offset by the benefit of fewer mutations being passed on. So how do mushrooms cope? They have evolved to avoid exchanging any mtDNA when they mate.

MITOCHONDRIAL DNA

In the early 20th century scientists found that certain animal and plant genes did not follow Mendel's laws of inheritance. They then found that these genes were not located on chromosomes. In fact, they were not even in the nucleus. These genes were present in organelles called mitochondria that provide energy for the cell.

Mitochondrial DNA (or mtDNA) is passed to young through just the female line. That is because the egg contributes all the mitochondria to the newly fertilized cell. The sperm has just enough mitochondria to get it to the egg but no more, and they are destroyed right after fertilization. Mitochondrial DNA mutates much more quickly than nuclear DNA does—mitochondria lack the suite of enzymes that iron out mistakes in the nucleus.

APPLICATIONS OF MTDNA

Mitochondrial DNA is used to trace family lines through the mother's side, and it has helped answer many questions about human history. For example, mtDNA has proved that Native Americans migrated from northern Asia to North America

VOLCANIC TORTOISES

Biologists have used DNA evidence to learn about the history of many species. Mutations in DNA occur at a regular, predictable rate and can be used as a kind of clock. The largest population of Galápagos giant tortoises lives on the slopes of a volcano called Alcedo on the island of Isabella in the Pacific. Genome studies of these tortoises reveal that they have very little genetic diversity. Known as a genetic bottleneck, this suggests that the tortoise population suffered a spectacular crash at some point in the past. By looking at modern levels of diversity, biologists have estimated that this crash took place around 100,000 years ago.

This ties in neatly with geological evidence. Also around 100,000 years ago Alcedo erupted explosively. The

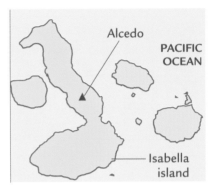

biologists suggest that the volcanic eruption killed almost all of the hapless tortoises, with just a few survivors. All the giant tortoises on the slopes today descend from these survivors.

in a single wave rather than in three as previously suggested. Similarly, mtDNA research has shown that all people of European descent are related to one of seven women from various parts of Europe. They lived between 10,000 and 45,000 years ago. Mitochondrial DNA was even used to prove that human remains found in the Ural Mountains in 1991 were those of the Russian royal family, who were executed in 1918.

Giant tortoises enjoy wallowing in the mud at the Alcedo volcano. The tortoises' genetic similarity suggests there was once a drastic reduction in the population.

CHAPTER SIX

CONCEPTS IN HUMAN GENETICS

Human chromosomes carry the genetic code. Genes drives cell development, but some can cause inherited diseases.

DNA, in the form of genes, directs the way that every cell in your body functions. Genes are inherited by children from their parents. The complete set of genes in a body cell is your genome. After many years of work scientists completed the Human Genome Project, or HGP, in 2003. That involved mapping the entire human genome. The HGP had important implications for treating genetic disorders.

CLOSEST RELATIVES

People have always considered the chimpanzee to be a close human relative, but research in 2003 showed just how close the relationship is. DNA evidence revealed that people and chimpanzees share 99.4 percent of their genetic material.

The scientists who conducted the research recommended that the two species of chimpanzees should be reclassified. They suggested moving chimpanzees from the genus (group) *Pan*, where they are currently placed, to the genus *Homo*, the same one as humans. Such a switch would be controversial.

It would raise many questions about how chimpanzees are treated in medical research and in the wild.

In genetic terms there is very little difference between this girl and her chimp friend.

23 IMPORTANT PAIRS

Every species of living organism has a certain number of chromosomes. They carry genes that form a code that determines the physical characteristics of the organism. Chromosomes are formed by coiled-up molecules of DNA. The number of chromosomes varies among species. Humans, for example, have 46 chromosomes, fruit flies have just 8, while one type of fern has 1,260!

Of the 46 human chromosomes, 44 can be arranged into pairs of similar size and structure; they are called homologous (matching) pairs. The remaining pair are called the sex

A person's sex depends on the combination of sex chromosomes received from their parents. When sperm are formed inside a man, some are X and others Y. Chance alone decides which type fertilizes a woman's egg.

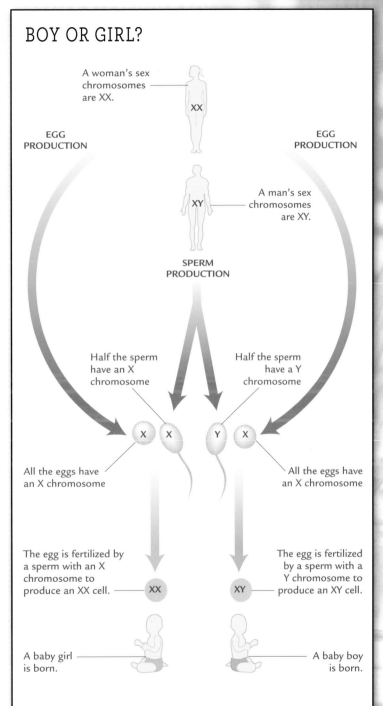

BOY OR GIRL?

A woman's sex chromosomes are XX.

XX

EGG PRODUCTION

EGG PRODUCTION

XY

A man's sex chromosomes are XY.

SPERM PRODUCTION

Half the sperm have an X chromosome

Half the sperm have a Y chromosome

X X

Y X

All the eggs have an X chromosome

All the eggs have an X chromosome

The egg is fertilized by a sperm with an X chromosome to produce an XX cell.

XX

XY

The egg is fertilized by a sperm with a Y chromosome to produce an XY cell.

A baby girl is born.

A baby boy is born.

NUMBER CHANGES

When stained, the chromosomes of different species sometimes have similar patterns of bands on them. This indicates that the species are related. The chromosomes of humans and apes (chimps, gorillas, and orangutans) have very similar banding patterns. However, humans have 46 chromosomes, but apes have a couple more, with 48. In one of our distant human ancestors, two pairs of chromosomes joined together to form one pair. That left our human ancestors with 46 chromosomes in total.

chromosomes. One of your sex chromosomes was provided by your mother and is called an X chromosome. The other member of this chromosome pair was provided by your father. It may be another X or a different, smaller chromosome that carries few genes, called a Y. If you are a girl, you received a pair of X chromosomes from your parents. If you are a boy, you got one X and one Y chromosome.

This arrangement of sex chromosomes has important implications for the inheritance of certain diseases. That is because many inherited diseases are linked to the X chromosome.

REPRODUCTIVE CELLS

The nucleus (control center) of most human cells contains a full set of 46 chromosomes. Cells with this full complement of chromosomes are known as diploid. Things are different in the sex cells—sperm in men and eggs in women.

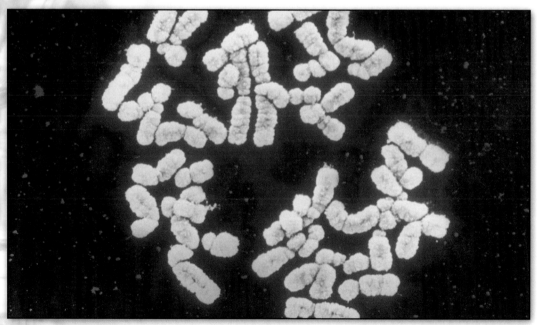

Human chromosomes under an electron microscope.

These children all have the same sorts of genes—that is what makes them human. However, the children do not look identical. That is because a variety of different alleles in different combinations are present.

BUILD YOUR FAMILY TREE

Draw your family tree on a piece of paper. Include yourself and any brothers and sisters, your parents, and your grandparents. For each member of the family record the presence or absence of an inherited characteristic, such as eye color, hair color, or color blindness. See if you can figure out how these characteristics have been inherited in your family through the generations.

These cells are produced by a type of cell division called meiosis. Meiosis leads to cells with 23 chromosomes, half as many as other cells in the body. Cells like these are called haploid cells. They become diploid again only if fertilization occurs.

Fertilization happens when a sperm penetrates an egg. Then the two haploid cells join, producing a cell called a zygote that has the full set of 46 chromosomes. This new diploid cell divides again and again to form an embryo. The embryo develops further and eventually grows into a baby.

IDENTICAL TWINS

Although everyone has the same types of genes, no two people look exactly the same. That is because genes have variants (different forms) called alleles. Even most twins do not look alike. Identical twins are the only exception to this rule. In this case a single sperm fertilizes an egg, just as in single births. However, the fertilized egg splits in two early in its development. This leads to two embryos growing in the uterus rather than one. The resulting pair of babies are genetically identical.

INHERITANCE OF TRAITS

Everybody has a unique combination of alleles. It is called a person's genotype. You inherited your genotype from your parents. Whether you have a feature of one parent or the other depends on the types of alleles you received from them.

Alleles come in two forms. Dominant

Though they look similar, these twins are not identical. We know that because one is a boy, and one is a girl; since identical twins have identical genes, they must be of the same sex.

alleles are always expressed regardless of what the other allele is. Recessive alleles are different. A recessive allele is expressed only if two copies of it are present; in other words, in the absence of a dominant allele. For example, the allele for brown eyes (B) is dominant. It masks the effect of the recessive allele for blue eyes (b). Similarly, the allele for brown hair (H) is dominant, while the fair hair allele is recessive (h).

Features of a child also depend on the allele combinations of their parents. Sometimes both alleles of a gene are identical. They are called homozygous alleles. Different alleles in a pair are called heterozygous alleles.

Imagine a man who is homozygous for both brown hair and blue eyes (HHbb). His wife is homozygous for fair hair and brown eyes (hhBB). All their children will have brown hair and brown eyes because the alleles that code for these

characteristics are dominant. However, all the children will be heterozygous for these features—in other words, their genotype will be HhBb. That is because they will have inherited recessive alleles for fair hair and blue eyes (h and b) as well as the dominant varieties (H and B) that are expressed.

SEX-LINKED GENES

Genes that are carried by the sex chromosomes are called sex-linked. You might think that characteristics more common in men are the result of genes that lie on the Y chromosome. However, the Y chromosome has very few genes; instead, sex-linked genes are usually present on the X chromosome. Conditions such as hemophilia (a disorder of the blood) and color blindness are sex-linked traits. These conditions are caused by recessive alleles. Women are carriers—they pass on a condition but only rarely have it themselves. That is because women have a second X chromosome that usually contains a dominant, healthy allele.

It masks the effects of the recessive version. Men are much more likely to suffer from a sex-linked disorder than women are. The Y chromosome does not provide a dominant allele to compensate for a recessive allele on the X chromosome.

A famous example of a sex-linked trait is hemophilia, which occurred in various European royal families from the

GENETIC TESTING

Genetic testing allows high-risk individuals to find out whether or not they are carriers of certain inherited diseases. For example, people who are considered at high risk for Alzheimer's disease—which causes loss of memory and thinking ability in older people—can be tested. However, at present the results are inconclusive; people who test positive for the condition do not always suffer from it in later life.

DIAGNOSING COLOR BLINDNESS

Take a look at this picture. What do you see? You can probably see the number 8 in bright red, surrounded by darker red dots. However, if you are color-blind, you will be unable to make out the number. This is called an Ishihara test. It is a good way to find out if a child is color blind. Color blindness is caused by a recessive sex-linked allele. Women can act as carriers for this allele. To suffer from the disorder, a woman must inherit two copies of the recessive allele—a rare event. Men, on the other hand, are far more likely to be sufferers. They do not have a second X chromosome on which a dominant allele can occur.

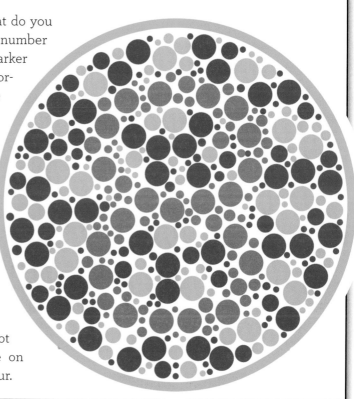

19th century onward. Queen Victoria (r. 1837–1901) of Britain inherited the recessive allele. She transmitted it to her son Leopold (1853–84), who suffered from hemophilia. Victoria had several daughters who were carriers of the allele. As they married into other European royal families, more hemophiliac princes were born.

Sex-linked conditions like hemophilia cannot be passed from father to son because the father's X chromosome is passed only to daughters.

GENETIC DISEASES

In the late 1890s, British physician Archibald Garrod (1857–1936) suggested that genetic defects caused inherited diseases. The importance of his observations was not truly appreciated until after 1953, when the structure of DNA was discovered. Disease can also be caused by poor diet or infectious organisms, but about 4,000 diseases are the result of inherited disorders.

Queen Victoria (*center*) with her family, including children, grandchildren, and great-grandchildren. A number of these relatives carried the hemophilia gene.

Some genetic diseases, such as cystic fibrosis, are caused when recessive alleles are inherited from both parents. Cystic fibrosis causes, among other symptoms, serious breathing difficulties.

The gene responsible occurs on chromosome 7. A disorder called Tay-Sachs disease is caused by the body's failure to produce a key brain protein, leading to death at around age 4. Most common in children of European Jewish ancestry, Tay-Sachs disease is caused by a mutation to a gene on chromosome 15.

How the gene for hemophilia ran through one branch of Queen Victoria's descendants. The gene passed into the Russian royal family through Victoria's granddaughter, Princess Alexandra of Hesse.

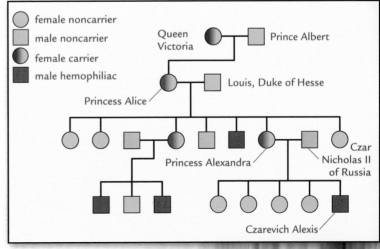

CHROMOSOMAL DISORDERS

Some genetic diseases are not inherited but are caused by problems with the number of chromosomes present. Down syndrome is caused by the presence of an extra copy of chromosome 21. People with this condition have 47 chromosomes in their cells rather than the usual 46. Sufferers of Klinefelter's syndrome have more sex chromosomes than normal. Instead of having two sex chromosomes (XX or XY), sufferers have three—they can be XXY or XYY. People with another disorder, Turner's syndrome, have only one sex chromosome (XO).

DIAGNOSIS IN THE UTERUS

Amniocentesis is a prenatal (before-birth) technique. It is used to examine the chromosomes of a fetus (developing baby). Physicians remove a small amount of the fluid that surrounds the fetus in the mother's uterus. The fluid contains fetal cells. The cells can be tested to find out if the fetus has any genetic problems. Amniocentesis is often offered to pregnant women who are more than 35 years old to check for Down syndrome. The test also allows the sex of the baby to be known at a much earlier stage than is otherwise possible.

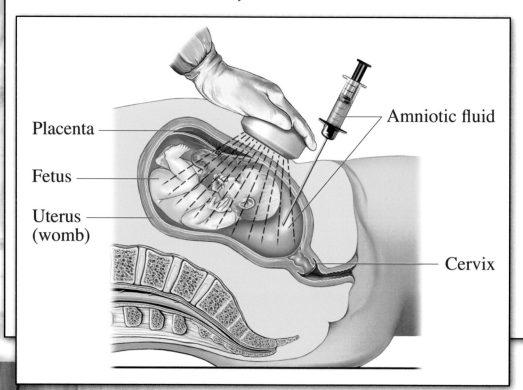

Placenta

Fetus

Uterus (womb)

Amniotic fluid

Cervix

MAPPING GENES

Many traits are determined by a single gene. Physicians can trace the inheritance of such a gene by looking at a family tree. That allows them to see how the gene has been transmitted and to guess what might happen in future generations. This type of gene mapping is commonly used when investigating congenital illnesses (illnesses that are present at birth).

Scientist Sir John Sulston is preparing samples during work on the Human Genome Project.

HGP SEQUENCES HUMAN DNA

In the mid-1980s scientists put forward the idea of the Human Genome Project (HGP). It would involve figuring out the complete human DNA sequence—a massive task. More than 20,000 genes would have to be found (at the time, scientists believed there would be even more), and sequences of the 3 billion base pairs that make up human DNA would need to be figured out. Research began in 1990. The first results were published in 2000, and the project was finally completed in 2003.

The HGP cost around $3 billion, but there have been many benefits. For example, scientists can now figure out which genes are connected with which diseases. However,

HOW THE HGP CAN HELP

Hutchinson-Gilford progeria syndrome is an extremely rare genetic disorder. It causes aging to occur at around seven times the normal rate. Scientists think a small mutation on chromosome 1 causes the disorder. This recent discovery came from the HGP. By comparing DNA from children with the condition to that mapped out by the HGP, scientists have shown that the mutation is present in 90 percent of sufferers. This finding may one day lead to gene therapy techniques that can treat the disorder.

This boy has Hutchinson-Gilford progeria syndrome. Discoveries from the HGP may lead to the development of a treatment for this condition.

INTERFERENCE RNA

RNA, or ribonucleic acid, occurs inside cells and is important for producing proteins. Scientists have realized that a type of RNA called interference RNA, or RNAi, could be vital in the fight against some cancers. These cancers are caused by over-production of certain proteins. RNAi works by binding to RNA in the cell. That stops it from producing proteins, switching off the disease-causing gene.

HUMAN EVOLUTION

For many years the study of human evolution has been based on fossils—the remains or traces of long-dead creatures preserved in rocks. Bones from various ancient hominids allowed scientists to piece together our past, but there are many gaps in the fossil record. Scientists are now using DNA to trace our evolutionary origins.

For example, in 2002 biologists managed to extract small samples of DNA from the bones of a Neanderthal man. The DNA evidence suggested that these ancient folk, who disappeared around 30,000 years ago, were probably not the ancestors of any modern peoples.

some people worry about whether it is ethical (right) to have such information about a person's DNA. What might be done with the data? How might insurance companies and employers deal with people who are at risk of developing certain diseases?

As scientists learn more about human genetics, the number of such ethical issues also increases. There is still much to be investigated; we still know little about genetics and the aging process, for example, while the genomes of almost all other organisms remain to be explored.

CHAPTER SEVEN

APPLYING GENETIC KNOWLEDGE

Scientists apply knowledge about genetics to create useful products.

Farmers have selected and bred animals and plants for their useful qualities since ancient times. Early farmers sowed wheat plants and harvested them for their grain to make bread and other foods. They kept back seeds from the plants that gave the best harvest and sowed them the following year.

Over many generations wheat plants were produced that were very different from their wild ancestors. Choosing the best individuals of a crop and using them to produce the next generation is called

In this mural painting, an ancient Egyptian villager harvests wheat. Agriculture has been practiced for thousands of years. This painting dates from around 1300 BCE.

WONDERFUL WHEAT

Early farmers selected wheat strains with plump grains that stayed on the stem before harvesting. In the 20th century farmers began using combine harvesters to gather in the crop. These farmers favored strains that readily released the grain when it was threshed inside the harvester. Wild wheat contained two sets of chromosomes (packets of genes) like most other organisms. However, over centuries of domestication wheat strains came to contain four sets of chromosomes and then six.

These changes occurred due to the crossing of different types of wheats. Organisms with extra chromosome sets are called polyploids. Plant breeders favored polyploid wheats because they were fast-growing and produced large grains.

selective breeding. After many such breedings an organism is altered for human use, or domesticated. Hundreds of crop plants have been domesticated, such as corn, tomatoes, and potatoes.

SELECTIVE BREEDING

Many animals have also been domesticated. For example, cattle were domesticated from a wild ox called an aurochs, while pigs originate from wild boar. Animal breeders chose individuals with qualities they wanted, such as a calm nature, plentiful muscles, or a good milk yield. Individuals with such characteristics were then used for breeding. Selective breeding like this led to the different breeds of domesticated animals that occur today. People bred horses

Scarlet runner beans were domesticated thousands of years ago by the Anahuac people of Mexico. Ideal for growth in more northerly regions due to their resistance to frost, the biggest bean crops were selected by farmers for breeding. The plants were also bred for their flowers.

AVOIDING ALLERGIES

In 1996 one company's plans to insert a gene from the Brazil nut plant into soybeans was thwarted by researchers. Some people suffer from a severe allergic reaction to even tiny traces of nuts. The researchers discovered that the Brazil nut gene produced a protein that triggered this allergy. People eating the soy would have had no way of knowing that it contained the allergy-triggering protein.

for specific jobs, such as pulling carts or plows, or for riding. They reared dogs to ward off wild animals or for hunting, while sheep and goats provided wool, milk, and meat.

Plant breeders had advantages over animal breeders because many plants breed both sexually (by passing pollen from male to female flowers) and asexually (through the production of bulbs or through grafting). Breeders could use a plant's ability to reproduce sexually to create new strains by crossing different plants with the qualities they were looking for. Once they had created a successful plant strain, they could use asexual reproduction to make copies that were genetically identical, or clones.

CROSS-BREEDING PLANTS

Crossing a pair of similar plant types produces hybrids. Hybrids may show the best traits of both parent plants and grow better. Biologists call this effect hybrid vigor. To produce a seed, each parent provides a set of gene variants, or alleles. The combinations of alleles control how the new plant develops. Hybrid vigor may be caused by the masking of harmful recessive alleles provided by one parent by dominant alleles supplied by the other.

The new combinations of genes in hybrid plants may also lead to features that do not appear in either parent. They may include disease resistance or faster growth.

RECOMBINANT DNA PIONEERS

In 1973 U.S. biochemists Herbert Boyer (born 1936) and Stanley Cohen (born 1935) made the first recombinant DNA. They cut open plasmids of *Escherichia coli* bacteria using a restriction enzyme. Then they added a section of DNA from another plasmid and used ligase to join the two together to re-form the ring of DNA.

Sexual reproduction leads to the combinations of alleles being mixed up. So if growers allow hybrids to interbreed, hybrid vigor is soon lost. Many of the plants in garden stores are first-generation, or F1, hybrids.

GENETIC ENGINEERING

Genetic engineering is the use of technology to add to or alter the genetic material of organisms. It brings together genes from different species. Since the early 1980s genetic engineering has become a very big and lucrative business, especially in fields such as medicine and agriculture. In a common genetic engineering technique researchers insert useful genes into bacteria. The bacteria then manufacture the product of the inserted genes. This process involves recombinant DNA technology—joining together DNA (genetic material) from separate sources.

The starting point for genetic engineering is often a bacterial plasmid. It is a ring of DNA that is separate from a bacterium's main batch of DNA.

THE RECOMBINANT DNA TECHNIQUE

plasmid — 1   restriction enzyme   2   cut ends of plasmid DNA

1. A restriction enzyme is mixed with a plasmid.

2. The restriction enzyme snips the plasmid DNA ring.

3   DNA sequence

3. A section of DNA is taken from another source, such as another plasmid.

4   DNA ligase

4. The new DNA is added to the plasmid, together with another enzyme, DNA ligase.

plasmid with inserted DNA   5

5. The DNA ligase joins the new DNA sequence to the plasmid and completes the ring. The plasmid is now recombinant DNA.

Genetic engineers use chemicals called restriction enzymes (for cutting into the DNA) and ligases (for joining it up again) to insert new genes into the plasmid. That produces recombinant DNA. The bacterium takes up the modified plasmid in a process called transformation. The genetic machinery of the bacterium then begins to produce the product coded for by the new genes.

Plasmids do not provide the only method for getting new genes into bacteria. Viruses called phages are sometimes used. Phages can insert longer stretches of DNA into bacteria, and takeup of the genes is usually more successful.

GENETIC ENGINEERING IN AGRICULTURE

Since the 1980s scientists have created many thousands of genetically engineered products for the agriculture industry. Genetically engineered plants that grow faster, have higher yields, and are resistant to pests such as insects offer obvious benefits to farmers.

ENGINEERED PEST KILLERS

An early genetic engineering success involved inserting into potato plants genes for an insect-killing poison produced by bacteria. The poison is made in the leaves of the engineered plants. It then kills off beetles, caterpillars, and other insect pests. When the plant dies and the leaves break down in the soil, the poison breaks down, too. Plant breeders have also engineered soy, potato, tomato, and many other types of food plants to be resistant to specific herbicides (weed killers). That allows farmers to spray herbicides on their fields to kill off weeds while leaving crops unharmed.

The Colorado potato beetle is a pest that can be controlled with genetically engineered plants.

Researchers are also testing the possibility of engineering crop plants that can grow in extreme conditions such as hot deserts and salt-rich soils.

MANUFACTURING DRUGS

DNA technology is also used by pharmaceutical companies to make medically useful substances. An early success was genetically engineered insulin, which the Food and Drug Administration (FDA) cleared for use in 1982.

Type I diabetes is a disorder in which the pancreas, an organ that lies in a fold of the large intestine, stops producing insulin. Insulin regulates the amount of sugar in the blood by driving its uptake

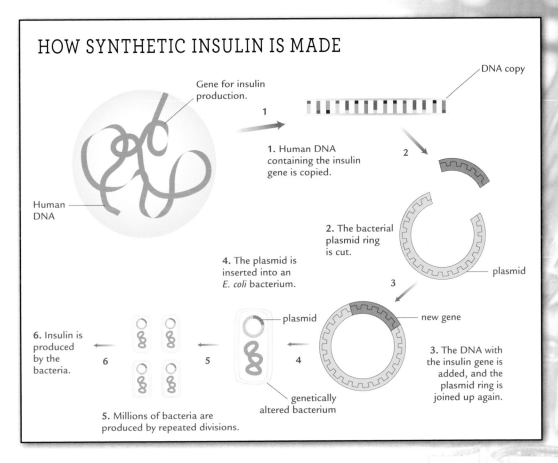

HOW SYNTHETIC INSULIN IS MADE

Gene for insulin production.

DNA copy

1. Human DNA containing the insulin gene is copied.

Human DNA

2. The bacterial plasmid ring is cut.

plasmid

4. The plasmid is inserted into an *E. coli* bacterium.

new gene

3. The DNA with the insulin gene is added, and the plasmid ring is joined up again.

6. Insulin is produced by the bacteria.

plasmid

genetically altered bacterium

5. Millions of bacteria are produced by repeated divisions.

To make human insulin using bacteria, scientists must first make a copy of the gene from a human's DNA (1). Then the ring of a bacterial plasmid is snipped using enzymes (2). The gene copy is inserted into the plasmid. The plasmid ring is re-formed, again using enzymes (3). The plasmid is then inserted into an *E. coli* bacterium (4). The bacterium divides to produce millions of insulin-producing bacteria (5).

FEATS OF ENGINEERING

Since the breakthrough with insulin production many other substances have been made using genetically engineered organisms. For example, some *E. coli* strains have been created to produce interferon. Human body cells use this chemical to combat infecting viruses. It is not just bacteria that are altered. Drug companies produce engineered sheep that contain genes for human growth hormone. Scientists harvest the hormone from the milk of the sheep.

into cells. Some diabetics must inject insulin to help control blood sugar levels.

Scientists used plasmids to add a human gene for making insulin to *Escherichia coli* bacteria. They became insulin-producing factories, with one bacterium dividing to produce more than 1 million bacteria in just 24 hours. Insulin became much cheaper and supplies more reliable. The original source for insulin on which many diabetics relied, pig carcasses, was swiftly replaced.

New strains of roses are created by grafting a section of stem from one type onto another. Roses are also genetically engineered; blue roses have been produced by adding genes from cornflower plants.

POSSIBLE DANGERS

Many people are concerned about the dangers of genetic engineering. Altered bacteria could escape into the environment. There they could pass on modified genes to other organisms. Such bacteria rely on supplements that are available only in the laboratory. That reduces the chances of a successful escape.

Crop plants engineered to be herbicide-resistant could pass genes to wild species, creating superweeds that would not be vulnerable to weed killers. Similarly, if insect-killing genes in crops spread to other plants, some species of insects could soon become extinct. A series of insect extinctions would have a devastating impact on the ecological balance of an area.

Food products created by genetic engineering, or genetically modified (GM) foods, may have some unpredictable effects on food consumers. Interactions between new genes and those of a modified organism could alter some aspect of its cell biochemistry. The organism might then produce substances to which some people might be allergic.

PLANT CLONING

A clone is an asexually produced organism that is genetically identical to its single parent. Many plants clone naturally when they produce bulbs, tubers, or similar structures. They grow to become genetically identical versions of the parent plant. Plant breeders harness this ability when they take cuttings from plants. They grow rose bush cuttings in soil or graft fruit tree cuttings onto the trunk of an existing tree (often of a different strain) that already has well-established roots.

Some plants, however, cannot be cloned using these traditional methods. Plant breeders have sought ways to artificially clone such species. Oil palms can be cloned by taking cells from the plant's growth regions and culturing them (growing them under sterile conditions). The cell clumps divide again and again to create a continuous supply of cloned plants.

ANIMAL CLONING

In the 1990s scientists began cloning mammals. In 1996 Scottish scientists cloned a sheep from genetic material taken from the wall of an adult sheep's

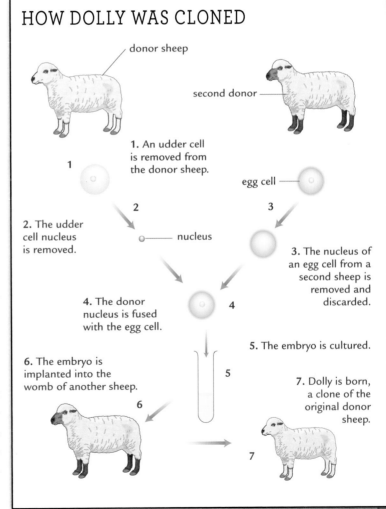

HOW DOLLY WAS CLONED

donor sheep

second donor

1. An udder cell is removed from the donor sheep.

egg cell

2. The udder cell nucleus is removed.

nucleus

3. The nucleus of an egg cell from a second sheep is removed and discarded.

4. The donor nucleus is fused with the egg cell.

5. The embryo is cultured.

6. The embryo is implanted into the womb of another sheep.

7. Dolly is born, a clone of the original donor sheep.

HUMAN CLONING

In 2003 several groups of scientists falsely claimed that they had cloned a human or were just about to do so.

It seems likely that human cloning will take place in the near future. Should people be trying to clone humans? What are the potential benefits, and what are the dangers? Begin with your own ideas. Then research reliable sources on the Internet to find the latest views on this controversial subject.

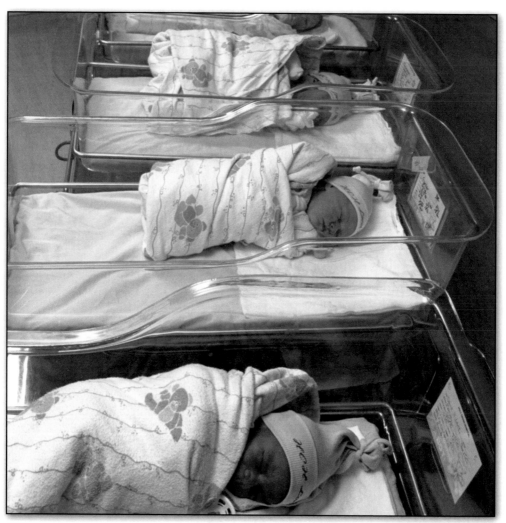

Will "baby farms" ever become a reality?

PROBLEMS WITH GENE THERAPY

Human gene therapy may one day revolutionize the treatment of inherited disorders. But various factors make it an extremely tricky process to undertake. Most human genes are large, and they are difficult to deliver to target cells. They usually work in concert with a host of other genes. Most importantly, the new genes must be accepted by the target cells before they are able to function.

GENE THERAPY FOR INHERITED DISEASES

Recently, medical scientists discovered how to alter the genes of people who have inherited diseases. This is called gene therapy. SCID is an inherited disease. The immune (self-defense) system of children with this disorder is unable to fight infections effectively. Such children can become seriously ill and die from infections that have little or no effect on most people. There are two forms of the illness. One is caused by the inheritance of a pair of recessive alleles, which can be controlled with regular injections of drugs. Gene therapy provides a longer-term answer. Early attempts in the 1990s

udder. They removed the nucleus (control center) containing the adult sheep's genetic material from the udder cell. They then put the nucleus into an egg cell that had also had its nucleus removed. The team implanted the resulting embryo into the uterus of a ewe, and the cloned lamb, Dolly, was born five months later.

Dolly was the result of the 277th attempt using that method—the previous 276 tries all failed. Since then researchers have cloned mice, goats, rats, and cattle using similar techniques. Animal cloning provides a way to ensure that offspring have desirable features found in their parents. However, the process also raises many moral and ethical concerns, especially since some rogue scientists are seeking to clone humans. Also, cloned animals may be likely to develop certain diseases. Dolly, for example, developed arthritis and died young.

THE POTENTIAL FOR GENE THERAPY

Despite slow progress so far, the outlook for gene therapy is very exciting. The human genome was sequenced in detail by 2003, and researchers have found dozens of genes involved in genetic disease. It is possible that gene therapy will one day treat many of the 4,000 or so known human genetic diseases. Gene therapy can also be used to treat diseases that are not necessarily inherited, such as certain forms of cancer. Genes inserted into cancerous cells could switch off the growth of the cell or could make the cells more sensitive to drugs designed to kill them.

proved only partially successful. But by 2002 a team of Italian and Israeli doctors had managed to establish a healthy immune system in two patients, who now lead normal lives.

The other, more common form occurs only in boys. It is caused by a mutation on the X chromosome and cannot be treated with injections. Sufferers have to live in an "air bubble" that keeps them away from as many infectious organisms as possible. Recent advances in gene therapy techniques by French scientists may help sufferers. The researchers take blood stem cells—cells that will eventually become blood cells but have yet to become them. Healthy genes are inserted into the stem cells. Then the cells are returned to the patient. So far nine boys have been treated. Most of them are healthy, although there are concerns that this treatment may lead to a high risk of leukemia.

FUTURE EFFORTS

Most of the gene therapies currently under research involve only the patient's nonreproductive body cells. Corrections to the genes of these cells cannot be passed on to children. However, gene

Wilco, the "bubble child" saved by Dr. Fischer's gene therapy in Paris, France, April 28, 2002.

THE SLIPPERY SLOPE?

Many people are concerned that tampering with human reproductive cells in germ-line therapy would alter the genetic destiny of entire families. Some see this approach to treating disease as a first step toward designer babies—a step they do not want to see taken. After all, they argue, if you can make your child disease free, why should it stop there? People might begin inserting genes for greater height or strength, features such as eye or skin color, or maybe even increased intelligence.

therapy would be more powerful if a person's reproductive cells could be treated. This process is called germ-line therapy. A mother or father with genes for a known genetic disorder could receive germ-line therapy. They would then know that they could not pass on the disorder to their children.

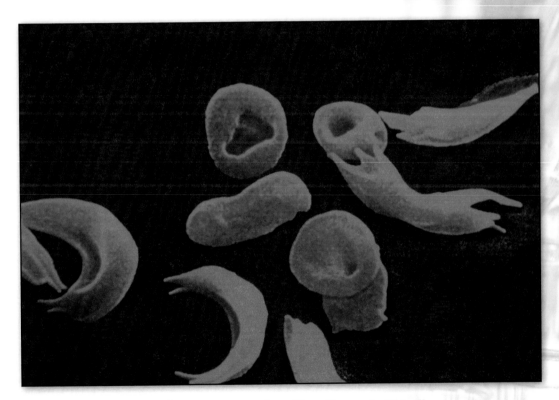

These are red blood cells from a person with sickle-cell anemia. This illness occurs in people who have inherited a pair of recessive genes. Scientists are trying to figure out gene therapies that will help treat this disorder.

CHAPTER EIGHT

BIOGRAPHY: GREGOR MENDEL

More than 150 years ago, Gregor Mendel, an Austrian monk, carried out detailed investigations into the way inherited characteristics are passed on to the next generation in plants. Although the significance of his research was not recognized until 16 years after his death, his studies led to the discovery of the units of inheritance, "genes," and laid the foundations for the study of genetics.

Johann Mendel was born on July 22, 1822; he later changed his first name to Gregor. He grew up in the town that was then called Heizendorf, in Silesia, which was part of Austria. It is now called Hynčice and is in the Czech Republic. His parents, Anton and Rosine, were

"My scientific work has brought me a great deal of satisfaction, and I am convinced that it will not be long before the whole world acknowledges [this effort]."
GREGOR MENDEL

This photograph shows the monastery garden in Brno, where Mendel performed his breeding experiments.

farmers; it was life on the family farm that first stimulated Mendel's interest in agriculture, horticulture, and botany.

Mendel went to the local school, and it soon became obvious that he was very intelligent. In 1841 he enrolled at the Philosophical Institute in Olmütz (now Olomouc), hoping to become a teacher. The family could not afford to keep him there, however. A farming accident in 1838 had left Mendel's father unable to work, and several poor

KEY DATES	
1822	Born in Heizendorf (now Hynčice) on July 22
1841	Enrolls at the Philosophical Institute in Olmütz (now Olomouc)
1843	Enters the Augustinian monastery in Brünn (now Brno), Moravia, taking the name Gregor
1847	Ordained as a priest
1849	Teaches Greek and mathematics in the school at Znaim (now Znojmo)
1850	Takes the examination for a teaching certificate, but fails
1851	Begins studying at the University of Vienna
1854	Returns to the monastery and begins to teach natural science at the technical high school in Brünn
1856	Begins breeding experiments with peas
1862	Natural history society founded by monks in Brünn
1865	Presents experimental results to the natural history society on February 8 and March 8
1866	Publishes results of his work in "Experiments with Plant Hybrids"
1868	Elected abbot of the monastery
1884	Dies at Brünn on January 6

harvests had meant that the family had been forced to spend their savings. As the only son, Mendel would have been expected to return home and take on the farm, but he did not want to do this. Instead he joined the priesthood, which would "free him from the bitter struggle for existence," and allow him to continue studying science. In 1843 Mendel entered the Augustinian monastery in Brünn (now Brno), taking the name of Gregor.

A GROWING INTEREST IN SCIENCE

During the 19th century there was a great growth of interest in the natural sciences. Natural sciences are those that involve the study of the physical world and everything in it, such as biology and geology. Scientists had begun to recognize the importance of communicating their work to the public, and the public seemed keen to hear their ideas. It became common for leading citizens to set up local societies to encourage scientific research.

Among those who tried to encourage an interest in science was C. F. Napp, abbot of the Brünn monastery. The monastery became a scientific institution as well as a religious one; it had a well-stocked library and provided an excellent environment for study. Abbot Napp warmed to Mendel's enthusiasm and intelligence, and welcomed him in.

Mendel continued to study science while he was preparing for the priesthood.

He was ordained in 1847. For a short time in 1849 he taught Greek and mathematics in a local school, and in 1850 he took the examination for a teaching certificate, but curiously, he failed, getting especially low marks in biology and geology.

Abbot Napp sent the young priest to the University of Vienna where, from 1851 until 1853, Mendel studied a wide range of scientific subjects.

In 1854 he returned to the monastery, but also began teaching natural science at the high school in Brünn. He taught there for a further 14 years.

WITH PEA PLANTS

At this time Brünn was an important center of the textile industry. However, the high-quality wool that was needed for its product was not available locally, and so had to be imported from Spain. This was an expensive business. People began to think about how they might improve the local sheep breeds in order to obtain better-quality wool. They set up breeding programs, but these were unreliable because no one was sure how to make the next generation inherit the most desirable characteristics of the previous one. It was against this background that Mendel began his breeding experiments with peas.

In early 1865 Mendel presented his results to a natural history society founded by his fellow monks. His results were published in 1866 as an article called "Experiments with Plant Hybrids."

EXPERIMENTS IN MENDEL'S GARDEN

Before Mendel's experiments, people believed in the principle of "blending inheritance." Taking hair color as an example, "blending inheritance" seemed to explain why children do not always have the same color of hair as their parents. A child who has one parent with fair hair and one with dark hair may have hair of an in-between shade. The theory of blending inheritance assumed that one parent contributed the characteristic for fair hair, the other the characteristic for dark hair, and the two merged to yield a blend. Mendel showed this was incorrect.

Mendel studied the color of pea flowers, which can be purple or white. He reasoned that, if the theory of blending inheritance were correct, when a plant with purple flowers was crossed with a plant with white flowers the offspring should have pale purple flowers. This would mean that after a time all pea plants would have pale purple flowers, and the strongly purple flowers and pure white flowers would disappear. However, this is not what happens. Pea plants continue to have either purple flowers or white flowers.

COMMON GARDEN PEAS

Mendel derived his laws of heredity from experiments he performed with edible peas (*Pisum sativum*), which he grew in the garden of the monastery. Pea flowers have petals that almost completely enclose the male and female reproductive organs (the stamens and carpel) and ordinarily the flowers pollinate themselves as pollen falls from the stamens onto the carpel. However, Mendel wanted to see what would happen if, for example, he pollinated a short plant with pollen from a tall plant.

Because of its structure, the edible pea plant was ideal for Mendel's experiments; he kept detailed records of his experiments.

In order to "cross-pollinate," Mendel first chose plants that bred true, which means that when they produced seeds in the usual manner by self-pollination, all those seeds would grow into plants that were identical to the parents. His experiments then involved cross-fertilizing between plants that bred true for different versions of the characteristics he was wanting to examine. So when studying flower color, for example, Mendel would cross plants that always produced purple flowers with plants that always produced white flowers.

Cross-pollination was a delicate operation. Mendel first removed the stamens from one set of plants before they produced pollen, leaving just the carpels.

He then used an artist's fine paintbrush to collect pollen from other plants

A single gene governs flower color in peas. It exists in two forms, or alleles: purple (P) and white (w). The allele for purple is dominant and the allele for white is recessive. This means that whether a plant inherits a purple and a white allele (Pw) or two purple alleles (PP), its flower color will still be purple. Only two white alleles (ww) will result in white flowers. The diagram shows what happens when a purple-flowered plant (PP) is crossed with a white-flowered plant (ww). The first generation (F1) all have purple flowers, but flowers in the second generation (F2) are purple or white in a ratio of 3:1.

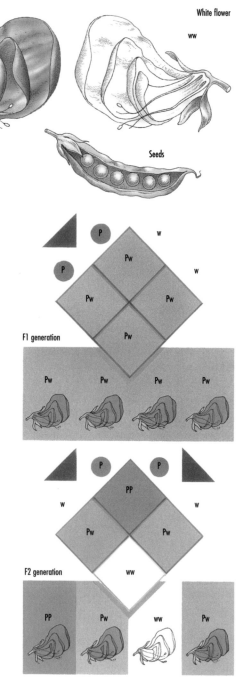

Purple flower PP

White flower ww

Seeds

F1 generation

F2 generation

and dust it onto those carpels. In this way Mendel could always be certain of the parentage of the seeds (peas) that were produced. Plants that are cross-fertilized in this way are called "hybrids."

In other experiments Mendel crossed plants that produce their flowers from different parts of the stem. He also studied the color of the seeds (yellow or green), the color of the pods (yellow or green), whether the plants were tall or short, whether the pods were smooth or whether they fitted tightly with the shape of the peas showing through, and whether the peas were smooth or wrinkled.

Using very large numbers of plants, Mendel would begin by painstakingly cross-fertilizing plants with two forms of whichever characteristic he was studying. He planted the seeds that were produced, and these grew into the "first filial" (F1) generation. He allowed the F1 plants to reproduce by self-fertilization, and then planted the seeds they produced to yield a second set of plants, called the F2 generation.

Mendel kept detailed records of the plants in each of the three generations. When the breeding experiments were complete he evaluated the results mathematically. In the case of flower color, for example, he found that in the F1 generation all the flowers were purple and that, out of the F2 generation, 705 of the plants had purple flowers and 244 had white flowers. This was a ratio of roughly 3:1. This same ratio appeared for all the characteristics he examined. Mendel reasoned that—for every characteristic they display—plants inherit two versions of what he called "heritable factors:" these are now known as "genes." If the plant inherited two factors that carried the same characteristic—purple flowers, for example— then the plant would have purple flowers. But if the plant inherited two different factors, one of these would dominate. So Mendel called one of the factors "dominant" and the other "recessive." In his color experiments the purple flower was dominant and the white flower was the recessive.

MATHEMATICAL PROOF

Mendel explained his laws using mathematics. If the dominant factor is called P and the recessive is w, then, using two parents that are known to breed true, PP crossed with ww gives plants that are Pw or wP. Since P is dominant, all the plants in this generation (the F1 generation) will exhibit the P factor.

The F2 generation is produced by crossing two F1 plants (Pw and wP). This yields plants that have Pw + PP + wP + ww. So three of these will exhibit the P factor and one will exhibit the w factor—which confirms Mendel's 3:1 ratio.

A visitor explores an exhibit on the pioneering work of Gregor Mendel at the Academy of Natural Sciences in Philadelphia.

Copies of this reached all the important scientific libraries in America and Europe, but it aroused no interest. Mendel also sent a copy to the leading Swiss botanist Karl Wilhelm von Nägeli (1817–1891), professor of botany at the University of Munich. Nägeli read the paper but apparently failed to appreciate the implications of the work. Years later Nägeli wrote a book on evolution but did not mention Mendel.

OF INHERITANCE LAWS

Mendel's study of inheritance revealed two general principles, now known as Mendel's Laws of Segregation and Independent Assortment. The Law of Segregation states that each inherited characteristic (or gene) is made up of two factors, one derived from each parent. Today these factors are called "alleles." For example, pea flowers may be purple or white, so there is an allele for purple flowers and an allele for white flowers. One allele is "dominant" and the other "recessive." In the case of pea flowers, purple is dominant and white is recessive. This can be written as capital P (dominant) and lower-case w (recessive).

When two dominant alleles are present, the characteristic associated with the dominant allele will be inherited; if a dominant allele and a recessive allele are present, the characteristic associated with the dominant allele will still be the one passed on. For example, a pea plant with Pw or PP will have purple flowers. Only if both alleles are recessive (ww) will the plant have white flowers. Mendel's Law of Independent Assortment states that characteristics are inherited individually, not as packages. So, for example, the color of the peas (yellow or green) and their shape (smooth or wrinkled) are inherited independently of each other.

So peas can be smooth and yellow, wrinkled and yellow, smooth and green, or wrinkled and green.

THE THEORY OF NATURAL SELECTION

About the same time as Mendel was experimenting with peas, English naturalists Charles Darwin (1809–1882) and Alfred Russel Wallace (1823–1913) were (separately) working out the theory of evolution by natural selection.

They had both noticed that all individuals vary slightly. They had also seen that, within a particular habitat (the natural home of an animal or plant), some variations give the individuals that possessed them an advantage when it comes to reproduction.

The individuals that possess these advantages will survive in greater numbers than those that do not, and will pass them on to their offspring, so eventually individuals with

This portrait of Gregor Mendel was created in 1926, forty-two years after his death.

these advantages become predominant. This is "natural selection," and Darwin and Wallace showed it is what drives the way animals and plants develop over time, or "evolve." However, neither Darwin nor Wallace knew how variation in species occurred; it was Mendel's work on heredity that helped biologists understand how characteristics could be passed on. Mendel's results, published a few years after Darwin's *On the Origin of Species* (1859), could have lent support to Darwin's theory of natural selection. However, although a copy of Mendel's paper, written in German, was sent to Darwin, he never read it.

THE ABBOT MENDEL

In 1868 Mendel was elected abbot, or head, of the monastery. Although he remained interested in botany, meteorology, and beekeeping, his involvement in the day-to-day running of the monastery left him little time for research orteaching. He died at Brünn on January 6, 1884.

MENDEL'S WORK IS REDISCOVERED

In 1900, some 34 years after he had finished his experiments with plant hybrids, Mendel's work was rediscovered. Three scientists who were working independently on heredity (the transmission of characteristics from one generation to-another)—Dutch botanist Hugo de Vries (1848–1935), German botanist Karl Erich Correns (1864–1933), and Austrian botanist Erich Tschermak von Seysenegg (1872–1962)—all came across copies of Mendel's paper on peas and drew attention to it. Their own work seemed to confirm Mendel's belief that characteristics are inherited in a ratio of 3:1. British scientist William Bateson (1861–1926) translated the paper into English, and through his own studies of the inheritance of comb shape in fowl, showed that Mendelian ratios are found in animal crosses as well as plants. It was Bateson who introduced the term "genetics" to describe the science of heredity that Mendel had founded.

SCIENTIFIC BACKGROUND

Before 1845

English naturalist Charles Darwin (1809–1892) notes that different species of Galápagos Island finches seem to have developed from a single mainland-based ancestor

Animal and plant cells are described by German physiologist Theodor Schwann (1810–1882) and German botanist Matthias Schleiden (1804–1881)

1845

1850

1851 German botanist Wilhelm Hofmeister (1824–1877) discovers the "alternation of generations", that generations of mosses and ferns are alternately sexual and nonsexual

1849 American naturalist Luther Burbank (1849–1926) begins developing new plant varieties, including the Burbank potato, the Shasta daisy, and different varieties of plums and berries

1855

1856 Mendel begins his experimentation using pea plants

1858 Charles Darwin and Welsh naturalist Alfred Wallace (1823–1913) put forward their theory of natural selecton in a joint paper to the Linnean Society in London

1860

1859 Darwin publishes his great work, *On the Origin of Species By Means of Natural Selection*

1865 French botanist Charles Naudin (1815–1899) describes his "theory of disjunction," which correctly concludes that inheritance is not a blending process

1865

1866 Mendel publishes the results of his experiments in "Experiments with Plant Hybrids"

1870

1868 Darwin publishes *The Variation of Animals and Plants Under Domestication*, expanding on his theory of natural selection

1875 German botanist Eduard Strasburger (1844–1912) publishes *Cell Formation and Cell Division*, in which he lays down the basic principles of the study of plant cells

1875

1880

1882 German biologist Walther Flemming (1843–1915) publishes *Cell Substance, Nucleus, and Cell Division*, in which he describes chromosomes and mitosis (cell division)

1885

After 1885

1900 Dutch botanist Hugo de Vries (1848–1935) is among several botanists who rediscover Mendel's work on heredity

1926) writes a defence of Mendel's work and later coins the term "genetics"

1911 American biologist Thomas Hunt Morgan (1866–1945) identifies heritable factors as genes

1902 English geneticist William Bateson (1861–

POLITICAL AND CULTURAL BACKGROUND

1845 The failure of the potato crop on which so many European people are dependent leads to the death of 2.5 million people there from famine; Ireland is particularly hard hit

1848 As revolution sweeps France, King Louis-Philippe (1773–1850) is forced to abdicate; he flees to Britain, calling himself "Mr Smith"

1852 American writer Harriet Beecher Stowe (1811–1896) completes her antislavery novel, *Uncle Tom's Cabin*, which sells 300,000 copies in the United States alone

1851 The Great Exhibition is held in London's newly built Crystal Palace; it is the first world trade fair

1863 The American Civil War turns in favor of Union forces when they win victories at Gettysburg, Pennsylvania, and Vicksburg, Michigan, preventing an invasion of the North and gaining control of the Mississippi River

1860 Construction begins on the world's first underground railroad system, in London

1869 The Suez Canal in Egypt is opened. A vital trade route connecting the Red Sea with the eastern Mediterranean Sea, ships traveling east to west will no longer have to travel around the entire African continent

1870 United States oil magnate John Davison Rockefeller (1839–1937) founds the Standard Oil Company with his brother William (1841–1922)

1877 *Black Beauty, The Autobiography of a Horse*, by English novelist Anna Sewell (1820–1878), pleads for better treatment of horses; it will become a worldwide bestselling book

1885 A National Parks system begins in Canada with the establishment of a reserve in the Canadian Rocky Mountains; it will be called Banff National Park

1884 Fourteen nations meet at the Berlin Conference. In order to ease tensions over the "scramble" for colonies in Africa, they come to an agreement on dividing up the continent between European nations

allele Any of the alternative forms of a gene that may occur at a given point on a chromosome.

amino acid Nitrogen-containing molecule that is a building block of proteins.

base Molecule on DNA that binds to a complementary base on the other strand.

cell cycle A cell's life cycle.

centriole Structure in the cell that helps form the spindle.

centromere Midpoint on a chromosome where the chromatids are joined.

chromatid Structure containing DNA; two join to form a chromosome.

chromosome DNA-containing structure that forms by the joining of two identical chromatids during cell division.

clone Organism that is genetically identical to its parent and siblings.

crossing over Exchange of genetic material between chromosomes during meiosis.

cytokinesis The physical splitting of a cell during division.

cytoplasm Contents of a cell outside the nucleus.

deoxyribonucleic acid (DNA) Molecule that contains the genetic code for all cellular (nonvirus) organisms.

diploid Cell or organism that contains two sets of chromosomes.

DNA hybridization Process that compares similarities between DNA samples to figure out evolutionary relationships.

dominant allele Allele that is always expressed regardless of the nature of the other allele in a pair.

double helix Twisted ladderlike shape of a DNA molecule.

egg Haploid female sex cell.

enzyme Protein that speeds up chemical reactions inside an organism.

exon Coding section of DNA.

F1 generation The young produced by a pair of test organisms. Their young are called the F2 generation.

gene Section of DNA that codes for the structure of a protein.

gene therapy Treatment of a genetic disorder by implanting healthy genes.

genetic disorder Illness usually caused by recessive genes.

genetically modified organism Organism with genes artificially implanted into its genome.

genome All the genes present inside an organism.

genotype The genes in an organism that code for a certain phenotype.

growth factor Chemical that makes nearby cells begin division.

haploid A cell such as a sex cell (or, rarely, the cells of a whole organism, such as a male ant) that contains one set of chromosomes.

heterozygous pair When two alleles in a pair are different (one is dominant, and one is recessive).

homologous pair A matching pair of chromosomes.

homozygous pair When two alleles in a pair are the same (both dominant or recessive).

hormone Chemical messenger that regulates life processes inside the body.

hybrid vigor Phenomenon whereby the hybrid young of two species grow larger, faster, and produce more young than either parent species.

incomplete dominance When just one copy of a dominant allele cannot produce the complete phenotype.

inheritance The receiving of genes and their associated characteristics by young from their parents.

interphase Nondividing part of a cell's life cycle.

intron Section of noncoding DNA that separates exons.

junk DNA Very long sections of noncoding DNA that serve no apparent function.

karyotype A visual profile of an organism's chromosomes, arranged in order of size.

linked genes Genes that lie on the same chromosome.

locus Point on a chromosome at which a certain gene occurs.

meiosis Process of cell division that produces sex cells.

messenger RNA (mRNA) Chemical that takes the genetic code from DNA in the nucleus to the ribosomes, where it becomes a template for protein production.

mitosis Process of cell division that leads to the production of body cells.

mutation A change in a cell's DNA.

nucleotide Part of a DNA molecule, comprising a sugar, a phosphate group, and a base.

nucleus Organelle that contains a cell's DNA.

organelle Membrane-lined structures inside eukaryote cells, such as the nucleus.

phenotype A feature coded for by a gene.

plasmid Ring of bacterial DNA separate from the organism's main DNA.

pollen Powder produced by male flowers that contains male sex cells.

polymerase chain reaction Process by which tiny fragments of DNA are amplified to allow analysis.

polyploid Organism that contains more than two sets of chromosomes.

protein Molecule formed by amino acids in the ribosome.

recessive allele Allele that is only expressed when paired with an identical allele (not when paired with a dominant one).

replication Self-copying of a DNA molecule.

ribonucleic acid (RNA) Chemical similar to DNA involved in protein production.

ribosome Granule on which protein production occurs.

sex-linked condition Genetic disorder caused by the mutation of a gene on the X chromosome; usually affects only males.

sperm Haploid male sex cell.

spindle Cagelike structure that forms during cell division on which the chromosomes align and move.

tetrad Structure formed by two chromosomes during meiosis, where crossover takes place.

transcription The process of converting the coding sections of a DNA molecule into RNA.

transfer RNA (tRNA) Type of RNA that binds to amino acids and brings them to a ribosome for assembly into proteins.

triplet Set of three bases on mRNA that codes for a specific amino acid during protein production.

zygote An egg fertilized by a sperm that will develop into a new organism.

American Society of Human Genetics (ASHG)
9650 Rockville Pike
Bethesda, MD 20814-3998
(866) 486-4363
Web site: http://www.ashg.org
The ASHG is a professional organization for human genetics specialists. It serves human genetics professionals, health care providers, and the general public by providing forums to share research results, advance genetic research, enhance genetics education, promote genetic services, and support responsible social and scientific policies.

Canadian Association of Genetic Counsellors (CAGC)
P.O. Box 52083
Oakville, ON L6J 7N5
Canada
(905) 847-1363
Web site: https://cagc-accg.ca
The mission of the Canadian Association of Genetic Counsellors is to promote high standards of practice, encourage professional growth, and increase public awareness of the genetic counseling profession in Canada.

DNA Learning Center (DNALC)
334 Main Street
Cold Spring Harbor, NY 11724
(516) 367-5170
Web site: http://www.dnalc.org
The DNA Learning Center is the world's first science center devoted entirely to genetics education. It is an operating unit of Cold Spring Harbor Laboratory, an important center for molecular genetics research. DNALC's family of Web sites includes animations, scientist interviews, historical images, and more.

Museum of Science and Industry, Chicago
57th Street and Lake Shore Drive
Chicago, IL 60637
(773) 684-1414
Web site: http://www.msichicago.org
This museum offers nearly fourteen acres of hands-on exhibits designed to spark scientific inquiry and creativity. Its exhibit on genetics includes a baby chick hatchery, an interactive, 3-D human genome, and a live demonstration in which DNA is extracted from visitors' cheek cells.

National Human Genome Research Institute (NHGRI)
National Institutes of Health
31 Center Drive, MSC 2152
Building 31, Room 4B09
9000 Rockville Pike
Bethesda, MD 20892-2152
(301) 402-0911
Web site: http://www.genome.gov
The NHGRI contributed to the International Human Genome Project, which aimed to sequence the human genome. This project was successfully completed in April 2003. The institute's mission has expanded to include research on the

structure and function of the human genome and its role in health and disease.

Tech Museum of Innovation
201 South Market Street
San Jose, CA 95113
(408) 294-8324
Web site: http://genetics.thetech.org
In the Tech Health and Biotech Gallery at this museum, visitors can explore new advances in the field of genetics, and play the role of a genetic counselor, scientist, or policy maker. In the Wet Lab, visitors can become real-life genetic engineers and grow jellyfish bacteria. The museum's Web site offers a variety of resources on genetics.

WEB SITES

Due to the changing nature of Internet links, Rosen Publishing has developed an online list of Web sites related to the subject of this book. This site is updated regularly. Please use this link to access the list:

http://www.rosenlinks.com/CORE/Gene

Anderson, Michael. *A Closer Look at Genes and Genetic Engineering* (Introduction to Biology). New York, NY: Britannica Educational Publishing in association with Rosen Educational Services, 2012.

Ballen, Karen Gunnison. *Decoding Our DNA: Craig Venter vs. the Human Genome Project* (Scientific Rivalries and Scandals). Minneapolis, MN: Twenty-First Century Books, 2013.

Buckley, Don. *Cells and Heredity* (Interactive Science). Boston, MA: Pearson Education, 2011.

Einspruch, Andrew. *DNA Detectives* (Discovery Education). New York, NY: PowerKids Press, 2013.

Guttman, Burton S. *Genetics: The Code of Life* (Contemporary Issues). New York, NY: Rosen Publishing, 2011.

Day, Trevor. *Genetics: Investigating the Function of Genes and the Science of Heredity* (Scientific Pathways). New York, NY: Rosen Central, 2013.

Duke, Shirley Smith. *You Can't Wear These Genes* (Let's Explore Science). Vero Beach, FL: Rourke Publishing, 2011.

Gardner, Robert. *Genetics and Evolution Science Fair Projects* (Biology Science Projects Using the Scientific Method). Berkeley Heights, NJ: Enslow, 2010.

Hall, Linley Erin. *DNA and RNA* (Understanding Genetics). New York, NY: Rosen Publishing, 2011.

Heos, Bridget. *The Human Genome* (Understanding Genetics). New York, NY: Rosen Publishing, 2011.

O'Neal, Claire. *Projects in Genetics* (Life Science Projects for Kids). Hockessin, DE: Mitchell Lane, 2011.

Sandvold, Lynette Brent. *Genetics* (Big Ideas in Science). New York, NY: Marshall Cavendish Benchmark, 2010.

Stille, Darlene R. *Altering the Biological Blueprint: The Science of Genetic Engineering* (Headline Science). Mankato, MN: Compass Point Books, 2011.

Vaughan, Jenny. *Who Discovered DNA?* (Breakthroughs in Science and Technology). Mankato, MN: Arcturus Publishing, 2010.

Van Gorp, Lynn. *Gregor Mendel: Genetics Pioneer* (Mission: Science). Mankato, MN: CompassPoint Books, 2009.

PHOTO CREDITS